Running Tough

Michael Sandrock

Sports Writer, Boulder Daily Camera

Human Kinetics

Library of Congress Cataloging-in-Publication Data

Sandrock, Michael, 1958-
    Running tough / Michael Sandrock.
        p.   cm.
    ISBN 0-7360-2794-7
        1. Marathon running--Training. I. Title.

    GV1065.17.T3 S25   2001
    796.42'52--dc21

                                                    00-061465

ISBN: 0-7360-2794-7

Acquisitions Editor: Martin Barnard; **Managing Editor:** Melinda Graham; **Assistant Editor:** John Wentworth; **Copyeditor:** Lisa Morgan; **Proofreader:** Pam Johnson; **Graphic Designer:** Nancy Rasmus; **Graphic Artist:** Francine Hamerski; **Photo Manager:** Clark Brooks; **Cover Designer:** Jack W. Davis; **Photographer (cover):** Carmel Zucker; **Printer:** United Graphics

About the cover: Adam Goucher finishes an interval session at the Potts Field track in Boulder while training for the 2000 Olympic Games. Photo by Carmel Zucker.

Human Kinetics books are available at special discounts for bulk purchase. Special editions or book excerpts can also be created to specification. For details, contact the Special Sales Manager at Human Kinetics.

Printed in the United States of America   10 9 8 7 6 5 4 3 2 1

Human Kinetics
Web site: http://www.humankinetics.com

United States: Human Kinetics, P.O. Box 5076, Champaign, IL 61825-5076
800-747-4457
e-mail: humank@hkusa.com

Canada: Human Kinetics, 475 Devonshire Road Unit 100, Windsor, ON N8Y 2L5
800-465-7301 (in Canada only)
e-mail: humank@hkcanada.com

Europe: Human Kinetics, P.O. Box IW14, Leeds LS16 6TR, United Kingdom
+44 (0)113-278 1708
e-mail: humank@hkeurope.com

Australia: Human Kinetics, 57A Price Avenue, Lower Mitcham, South Australia 5062
(08) 82771555
e-mail: liahka@senet.com.au

New Zealand: Human Kinetics, P.O. Box 105-231, Auckland Central
09-309-1890
e-mail: humank@hknewz.com

Contents

Preface   v
Acknowledgments   xi
About the Photos   xiii

1 Long Runs: Building a Base   I

2 Off-Road Training: Sparing Your Legs   21

3 Fartlek Training: Mixing It Up   49

4 Interval Workouts: The Need for Speed   69

5 Hill Workouts: Building Strength and Stamina   107

6 Tempo Runs: Pushing the Threshold   125

7 Recovery Fun: Rejuvenating With Play   149

8 Building a Program: Preparing
for Competition   165

Workouts   197
About the Author   201

Preface

One dark, midwinter evening in early 1971, Steve Prefontaine and Frank Shorter were on a 10-mile training run high in the mountains outside of Taos, New Mexico. It was cold—the bitter, goes-right-through-you-like-a-knife kind of cold that often descends on the Rockies like a sheet of ice after the sun goes down.

There was no spandex back then, no Lycra, no polypropylene tights, no shoes with air or gel in the soles, no heart rate monitors or digital watches. Those of you who have run in such conditions know that the winter wind bites right through those flimsy, antediluvian nylon tops we used to wear, and once the wetness freezes, your legs and arms numb up. You can't see because sleet and snow are blowing directly into your face, crusting up and freezing your eyelids and turning you into a snowman—or snowrunner, in this case.

It was Shorter's and Prefontaine's second run of the day, and it came after a full afternoon of skiing on the difficult, double black-diamond slopes of Taos Mountain. The two runners were freezing, tired, and cranky. "Frank, this is crazy. Let's head back, light a fire, and have some dinner," Prefontaine said through the ice hanging from his mustache and eyebrows.

Shorter looked over at his friend, squinted into the blinding snow, and said, "Steve, no one is training as hard as we are right now. No one." With that, the duo put their heads down and finished the run, warmed only by the knowledge that they were doing the best training they possibly could.

Maybe Shorter was right. Perhaps he and Prefontaine were training better than anyone else in the world just then, better than Lasse Viren or Juha "the Cruel" Väätäinen in Finland, Mamo Wolde and Miruts Yifter in Ethiopia, Derek Clayton in Australia, Kip Keino in Kenya, or Brits Ron Hill, Ian Thompson, and David Bedford. There is no way to know for sure, but we do know that few people in the early 1970s were putting in 170-mile weeks at high altitude as Shorter sometimes did, along with fast track sessions. What is just as important is that Shorter believed he was doing the best possible training he could, training developed through his collegiate years at Yale under Olympic coach Bob Giegenack and later with Jack Bacheler and the Florida Track Club.

Shorter's faith that he was training better and harder than any of the world-class runners he would be facing in the Munich Olympic Games filled him with confidence—a confidence that helped him do the workouts necessary to win two Olympic medals.

Shorter always had a simple concept of training when he was among the best runners in the world. He trained twice a day, with one long run and two or three interval sessions a week. He was smart enough to listen to people like Giegenack and Bacheler, keeping what he found good about their training and melding it into his own program.

All great runners have their favorite workouts. These are their signatures, their personal flourishes. The workouts differ as much as the personalities of the athletes. The erudite, smooth-striding Shorter loved running intervals on an indoor track in a dilapidated fieldhouse; the fiery Said Aouita busted run-to-your-limit 400-meters; Steve Cram liked to do 300-meter intervals; Steve Jones favored fartlek sessions on the grass, and the laid-back Rob de Castella enjoyed hill sprints and long runs.

It is a mystery why certain workouts become an athlete's favorite. They are as personal as your favorite artist, the music you listen to, what you wear, your choice of careers, even what you like to eat in the morning.

Most runners start out running easy. After a while, months for some, years for others, the urge to get faster builds. But how do you go about getting faster? What workouts should you do? Long or short? Intervals or fartlek? Should you run on the roads or the track? What I offer here are workout sessions that have worked for a cross section of runners, along with the runners' reasons for doing them. I'm not suggesting that you can, would want to, or even could, do them all. In fact, perhaps I should put a label on the front of this book, reading "Warning: do not try these workouts at home without the help of a trained professional. Dilute them before use."

Although you likely will not be able to run Prefontaine's 40-30 workout on the track for more than a couple of laps, you can do a similar workout based on the training principles formulated by Pre's coach, Bill Dellinger. A key point: just because somebody ran a 2:07 marathon doing some of these workouts does not mean you will be able to do the same. This is because we all have different amounts of talent, ability, motivation, and time to train, and we all have different life situations. You are not Steve Prefontaine, Libbie Hickman, or Adam Goucher; nor were you likely meant to be. You are, however, a 2:30 or 3:40 marathoner, a 35- or 45-minute 10K or 16- or 19-minute 5K runner . . . and you can still find much benefit in these workouts.

This book is written for those of you interested in preparing to run the best races you can. Some of these are, indeed, tough runs. But then, they have to be, because these runners have set world and national records and have won Olympic and World Championship medals. These sessions have worked for some of the best runners in the world, and they can work for you, too, if you take some of the ideas presented and apply them to your own training.

Your workouts, however, have to be part of a well-thought-out plan. You need to look long term and keep "putting money in the bank." As de Castella used to tell young runners asking for advice, "There are no short-cuts." If you do not get impatient or injured, and if you keep your training going week after week, month after month, and year after year, you will improve. That is a guarantee. But to run to your potential, you must find what Arthur Lydiard calls the correct recipe. What I am giving you here are some key ingredients. It is up to you to pick and choose from the mix and cook up a meal that satisfies your soul.

Another point: unless you travel to Kenya's Rift Valley, you can't run Kip Keino's Agony Hill, or the Fluorspar Hill favored by so many of the great Kenyan marathoners now winning races around the world. You can, however, find a hill near your home and find your own agony on it. When running your hill, you, too, like the Kenyans or Europeans or Australians across the globe, can daydream of winning that next race, beating that one nettlesome rival, or setting a personal best. And that, after all, is a big part of what being a runner is all about—having the consistency, longevity, and drive to continue striving to surpass your limits and run your best, no matter what your age, profession, or gender.

We all have different goals. Perhaps some of you out there dream of making your college team or becoming the number-one runner on your high school squad. Others of you might dream of placing in your age group in a local race, or of setting a personal best. A select few of you, blessed—or cursed—with a very special drive, might even want to dedicate your lives to running in the Olympics.

Most of us know we will never run in the Olympic Games. But we can have a goal just as worthy and just as important to us: running as well as we can for as long as we are able. That is where these workouts have their role. They can help you get the most out of your training and become the runner you were born to be—or, better yet, the runner you hammer, chisel, and forge yourself into.

We each start out in life like one of those huge blocks of Carrara marble Michelangelo was faced with at the start of one of his projects. Through years of work, helped along by a bit of luck, the runner and person that dwells within you emerges from that undifferentiated block of stone that is your potential. Most of us are like one of the Michelangelo sculptures called "The Captives," forever caught half-formed in the stone, struggling to be free. A few runners, however, end up like the great Florentine's "David": majestic, fully formed, fully human. These are the Deeks, Joneses, Salazars, Barrioses, Mollers, and Benoit-Samuelsons. But no matter how we end up, what a grand project we have embarked on, and what artists we have to be to shape and create ourselves in the process of freeing ourselves from that block of stone.

Of course, following the workouts of some of the top runners and coaches is not enough. To be the best requires that ineffable something extra only champions have: a fiery determination and perseverance that is hard to describe. You know it when you watch someone who has it. It is seen sometimes in photos of a Sebastian Coe, Haile Gebresallasie, or Hicham El Guerrouj concentrating on the last lap of a world-record race. It is that determination summed up by Arturo Barrios after winning a big road race while suffering from a bad flu: "I was either going to win the race or die." Those who have met Arturo know he was not joking.

Craig Masback, CEO of USA Track and Field, found out just what that determination is when he was a top miler running in meets on the European circuit in the summer of 1983. Between races, Masback was in Brighton, England, training with Steve Ovett. The two were getting ready for the Bislett Games mile in Oslo. One morning Ovett and Masback ran a ladder on the track consisting of 100 meters, 200, 300, 400, 300, 200, and 100 meters.

"The idea was to run faster on the way down than on the way up," recalls Masback. The times were quick, such as 37.8 seconds for the 300 meters and 50.6 for the 400. Masback was able to hang with Ovett until the final 200 meters. Then Masback hit the wall.

"You could see the whole difference between us in that one 200," said Masback, a 3:52.7 miler. "I was supposed to lead, but Ovett went right by me. I was so overloaded with lactic acid I could barely get across the line. Two weeks later Steve set the world record."

With that lesson in mind, what follows are a few of the most important workouts some top runners have used over the years. There are two reasons for providing them: first, the workouts are snapshots of a training program. You can review them and get some idea of the kind of work required to be among the best.

Second, maybe you will be able to incorporate one or more of these sessions into your own training schedule. You can modify them to suit your own lifestyle, living situation, and time constraints. You might not win an Olympic gold medal like Shorter did, or set eight American records like Prefontaine. I hope, however, that these workouts can help you become the runner you want to be and are capable of being. It will happen, sooner or later, if you keep your passion alive, stay healthy, and do the proper training.

What is the proper training? That depends on who you are, and sometimes it is easier to know what not to do than what to do. Top masters runner Craig Young ran 9:25 for 2 miles as a high school freshman and 9:06 as a sophomore, fast enough to break Craig Virgin's Illinois prep record. But Young did not improve after that, hindered by a schedule that had him and his teammates running intervals six days a week. With no warm-up. They would meet at the track, jump right into the intervals, then head directly to the shower. Needless to say, Young's early career was shortened by injury and lack of motivation. Somehow, however, Young kept his fire for running burning, and years after his prep days he finally improved on his sophomore personal bests and began winning races again. Here is how Young explained his drive:

"I love competing and pushing myself to the limits of my ability. I love working hard and improving. For me, the success I've achieved as a masters runner is redemption. I always believed that I had within me the ability to be one of the best in the world. It took years of frustration and hard work, but I never gave up on my dream. I hope I can serve as an example to others who have struggled and toiled under the burden of frustration to never give up. Believing in yourself and never giving up are the keys to success. Don't let anyone rob you of what is within you—the potential to become what your dreams beckon you to."

How can you fulfill your potential and realize your running dreams? By finding the proper training recipe and sticking with it. This book provides some of the ingredients of successful programs. It is up to you, or you and your coach, to find the right mix. The premise here is to provide a little of the theory behind the workouts, from the athletes or coaches themselves, along with their explanations of why these sessions work.

When training for a race, remember it is a question of being able to integrate your favorite workouts into your own program. Be patient, have a realistic plan, look long term, and let yourself recover from the workouts, no matter how long it takes at first. Some days you go out running with friends just to have some fun; other days—the workout days—you put on your game face and do your tough runs. And through the vicissitudes of our athletic lives, let us always keep in mind these wise words from New Zealand great Dick Quax: "There is no such thing as a magic workout. All training should reflect what we know about human exercise physiology and stay within those boundaries."

By coincidence, I am writing this in the same studio in Four Mile Canyon where I wrote *Running with the Legends*. Once again, looking out the window on a warm summer day, I see several lean, fit runners rolling up the canyon on what is known locally as the Poor Man's Loop. And once again, I am glad that new runners appear each year like wildflowers after a summer rain. Each of us runs alone in the end, yet also in the footsteps of all the runners who have preceded us through the years, stretching back to the inaugural Olympic Games back in 776 B.C.

When young runners in town ask me for advice, I tell them the same thing I leave you with now: keep up your training, keep having fun, and eschew the shortcuts, no matter how tempting they might look. That is what the runners in this book have done, and it is what I hope you do, too. Good luck, and happy running. I hope to see you on the roads, tracks, hills, grass fields, or woods—or wherever your favorite workout takes you.

Acknowledgments

I have to give my deepest thanks to my mother, Dorothy, for driving me to my first workouts back at Maine South High School, and my father, Albert, for buying me my first pair of training shoes (a pair of blue SL-72s). Several people at Human Kinetics deserve credit for having the patience to see this book to fruition, especially acquisitions editor Martin Barnard, who first came up with the idea, managing editor Melinda Graham, who patiently and with good humor pulled the disparate reams of information together, Nancy Rasmus, who gave the book its winning design, and Ted Miller, for hooking me up with HK in the first place when I wrote *Running with the Legends*.

As should be obvious, I had to bother a lot of runners to get the information in this book. My thanks goes out to all of them for being so willing to share their time and workouts. Several runners in particular were very helpful in exploring training theories, including Steve Jones, Lorraine Moller, Frank Shorter, Arturo Barrios, Rob de Castella, Shaun Creighton, Mark Wetmore, Fred Treseler, Benji Durden, George Zack, Andy Aiken, Scott Winston, Paul Christman, Marty Kibiloski, Peter Block, Kevin Koy, and Mark and Kevin Sandrock, who, while not yet elite runners, are world-class brothers. My training partners this past winter, Shannon Butler, Dan Skarda, Aaron Berthold, and Dave Smith, had to put up with a bit of whinjing (Aussie slang for complaining) now and then, as did my understanding sisters, Marguerite and Maura.

The sports editor at the *Daily Camera*, Dan Creedon, gave me time and space to write *Running Tough*, and Silvio Guerra and Melyssa Mooney took me salsa dancing, which can be quite a good anaerobic diversion. Friends such as Mimi Wesson, David Mastbaum, Pam Uhlenkamp, John and Carol Dowe, Bob Stone, and Brenda Cox lent me their ears, and the management at the Trident Cafe allowed me to sit for many hours in their lovely, book-laden cafe working and drinking genmaicha green tea until it was time for my next workout.

About the Photos

Chapter 1: Long Runs
U.S. runners Bryan Dunn, left, and Peter Hammer take an easy run outside of Eldoret, Kenya, in the winter of 2000. The pair spent a month training with some top Kenyan runners—and a giraffe or two. Photo by Victah Sailer.

Chapter 2: Off-Road Training
Libbie Hickman runs along Torrey Pines State Beach, outside of San Diego, during a March training camp before the 2000 track season. Hickman went on to make the finals of the Sydney Olympic 10,000 meters. Photo by Tim De Frisco.

Chapter 3: Fartlek Training
Steve Jones goes through a workout near the Royal Air Force base in South Glamorgan, Wales, not long after setting the marathon world record at Chicago in 1984. Jones worked full-time as a RAF mechanic while training for his record attempt.

Chapter 4: Interval Workout
Shawn Found, 2000 U.S. national 25K champion, leads Army runners Jason Stewart and Mike Bernstein during an interval workout of 6x1 kilometer before the 2000 Olympic trials. Found finished fourth in the 10,000 meters and Stewart placed seventh in the 5,000 meters at the trials. Photo by Jon Hatch.

Chapter 5: Hill Workouts
Alan and Shayne Culpepper run up a hill near the University of Colorado campus in the summer of 2000. Both Culpeppers raced in the Sydney Olympic Games. Photo by Michael Sandrock

Chapter 6: Tempo Runs
Two-time Boston Marathon winner Moses Tanui runs through a field near his Kaptagat training camp outside of Eldoret, Kenya. Photo by Victah Sailer.

Chapter 7: Recovery Fun
Ultra runner Adam Chase takes an easy run on one of his favorite trails along the Front Range of the Rocky Mountains. Photo by Cliff Grassmick.

Chapter 8: Building a Program
Olympic marathon bronze medalist Lorraine Moller raises her hands in celebration as she breaks the tape at the 1987 Osaka Marathon in Japan.

Chapter 1

Long Runs: Building a Base

Sometimes at the newspaper office where I work, the golf writer will make a comment when a race such as the Boston or the New York City Marathon is on TV. "How hard can running be?" he will invariably ask in a disparaging manner. "It's just left, right, left, right. It's so simple; there's nothing to it."

I never bother arguing with him, as it is not worth my while to talk with someone who would rather spend an afternoon driving a cart over some grass than running in a forest. But among friends, we can respond by saying, "Well, yes and no."

Running does indeed look simple and beautiful when the best athletes are gliding along smoothly at a 5-minute-mile pace. However, getting to the point where they can run their best race is far from simple, as most of you reading this book understand. There are myriad complex processes taking place in our bodies when we run that are truly wondrous and take years to cultivate.

"There is technique and skill involved in running. It's heaps more than just left foot, right foot," explains former marathon world-record holder Rob de Castella. "You have to be able to do this as efficiently as possible to conserve energy in the marathon and long races."

How do you learn the technique and skill of running? First of all, through your long runs. I put this chapter first because, according to Deek, Arthur Lydiard, Bill Rodgers, Steve Jones, and others, you have to be strong before you are fast. The importance of the long run cannot be overstated. It should be the foundation of your training and perhaps the key element in your training schedule because it develops your aerobic (*with oxygen*) system.

The great runners know this. That is why New Zealander Peter Snell ran 22 miles every Sunday over the Waiatarua mountains to prepare for his Olympic 800- and 1,500-meter gold medals.

Doing the long run week after week, month after month, year after year, is not easy. It is not as "sexy" as going to the track for intervals, and mentally gearing up for a long run is often more difficult than for a set of fast 200-meters. But beware: Those fast intervals will invariably lead to injury if your body has not been hardened and toughened enough by the long runs to handle them.

We live in an "instant" society, with instant fast food, instant diets (to lose the weight gained from the instant food), instant Internet, instant cell phones, pagers, e-mail, and 24-hour news. That outlook sometimes filters down to running. There are, however, no instant results in running. Seeking instant success typically leads to disaster. Better to steadily put in your long runs and look for far-off improvement. In fact, if you did nothing but long runs you would improve and be more likely to stay injury free. Our sport is a patient, long, and drawn-out affair that requires, above all—more than talent, altitude, or a new pair of shoes—determination, dedication, and discipline.

And the most dedication is required for the long runs.

- How long is a long run? That varies, depending on what race you are training for, your fitness level, and the time of year. However, we can classify a long run as anything over 90 minutes.

- How fast should you go on the long run? That, too, varies, depending on the runner. However, Jones and others say that the key point to keep in mind when planning your long run is this: The amount of time you spend on your feet is more important than your overall pace.

Worry about pace when you get to doing intervals or fartleks. On the long run, just get it in, consistently. A good measuring stick is that you should be able to talk during the entire distance. If you are going "eyeballs out" early in the long run, you are most likely going too fast, says Jones, also a former world-record holder in the marathon. And you run the risk of cutting your long run into a short run, which means you are not getting the important and often subtle benefits of the run.

What are the benefits of the long run? Let us count them. First of all, the long run is critical in preventing injuries. The long run provides the foundation, or base, that allows you to do faster, anaerobic workouts later on. Not laying a foundation means your training "house" will come crumbling down around you later on. Sometimes sooner, sometimes later, but it will happen.

This is because, as de Castella says, there are two aspects to racing well: strength and fitness. Injuries occur when your cardiovascular fitness exceeds your strength. When that happens, you are more apt to push your body past its structural limits. Long runs are the best way to prevent this from happening.

Look at it this way: Before you can put a racing engine in your car, you have to have a chassis, suspension, and drive shaft that can handle the higher speed. The long runs are what build that chassis. They strengthen your joints, tendons, ligaments, and muscles, laying the firm foundation that allows you to add speedwork onto your base without getting hurt.

More on strength and fitness: During a long run, your heart rate is elevated for an extended period. This stimulates the growth of new capillaries, the small blood vessels that over years of long running expand and grow through your legs like veins in a leaf.

In addition, the long run teaches your body to store as much glycogen as it can and to use that fuel efficiently. Finally, as de Castella points out, long runs also develop the motor neural pathways that fire all your muscles.

Have you ever seen a large and majestic conifer growing from a rocky cliff? At the cliff's edge you can see the tree's long, thick roots dangling down, going under and over rocks, searching the soil for nourishment. So it is with distance running. The long runs are the deep, thick roots that provide the nourishment for your fast training and keep your running progressing upright and true. The more long runs you do over the years, the deeper your roots and the more stable and secure your running.

The key to success in long-distance running, no matter what your level, is longevity, as nearly any champion will tell you. Do your long runs consistently and you will be more likely to run for a long time. Being a runner is about patience, perseverance, and enjoyment of what you are doing. The long run is the place to start on that journey for any runner.

Magnolia Never Lies

Mark Wetmore

University of Colorado head track and cross country coach
Four-time Big 12 or Big 8 Coach of the Year
Three-time District or Regional Cross Country Coach of the Year
Coach of 71 All-Americans and seven NCAA champions

The cornerstone of Wetmore's coaching is patient aerobic development. The most important workout in his program is what he calls "banging out," a solid 2-hour distance run every Sunday. This is not a jog, but a steady, up-tempo run. It is usually done on an old stagecoach and mining road called Magnolia Road. Magnolia is at 9,000 feet elevation with rolling hills in the mountains west of Boulder.

In the 19th century, it was the route to the gold fields of Central City and Blackhawk (the city that paved a sidewalk with gold bricks when President Ulysses S. Grant came for a visit). Now, Magnolia is the route to a different kind of gold for elite runners from around the world, ranging from Americans to Japanese to Kenyans.

Wetmore's approach to running can be described as slow and steady. His 2-hour Sunday run focuses on aerobic development and requires patience. Wetmore likes Magnolia because of its rolling hills and its difficulty. The Sunday Magnolia loop is not an easy run, something Wetmore feels strongly about.

"Some coaches say, 'Oh, go out and do a long run.' I say if you are just going out jogging you might as well be watching TV. This is a hard, long run."

Mark Wetmore

The rationale for this kind of workout is that doing the long run at a steady pace, without going anaerobic, advances the aerobic metabolism most efficiently, according to Wetmore. It gives you the most neuromuscular and capillary stimulus of the muscle groups being used. These benefits occur "when you are running too hard to talk about complicated subjects, but not too hard to talk in complete sentences. This is definitely born of (Arthur) Lydiard. Of course, you can lose your speed if all you do is one long run per week."

Stars like U.S. national cross country and track champions Adam Goucher and Alan Culpepper run their long runs at a 6-minute pace or less. Of course, the run on Magnolia cannot be so hard that Wetmore's athletes are not able to be ready for an interval session two days later.

Wetmore says these long runs are a good investment for any runner, NCAA or national champion or not. That is because, as mentioned previously, intervals are of greatest benefit when you run them after a solid aerobic foundation is laid. According to Wetmore, "In general, American runners are woefully unprepared from an aerobic standpoint."

Wetmore's advice for those of you with full-time jobs and not a lot of time in the week includes the following:

• The most important run you can do is the long, up-tempo Sunday run. If you are running 30 miles a week, of course you can't do 20 miles on Sunday, as his runners do, but you can do a 75- to 90-minute run.

As with his elite runners, make sure the Sunday run is not a jog. By *up-tempo,* Wetmore means a minute to a minute and a half slower than your 10K-race pace.

• Don't expect to see the results of your long runs overnight. Training requires patience. For instance, your training for a race on Memorial Day should really begin the previous July. Wetmore quotes Ken Cooper, author of *Aerobics:* "Americans spend 20 years getting out of shape and want to get in shape in 20 days."

If you are at the beginning of your running career, or just getting back to running, remember this insight from Wetmore: It takes 2 years for someone serious about training to get fit. A long run such as that on Magnolia Road is one of the best ways to increase your fitness.

2-hour up-tempo run

Recovery	A continuous run with no breaks
Pace	Around 6 minutes per mile for the elites; 1 to 1-1/2 minutes slower than your 10K personal best for other runners
When to do	Once a week
Total distance	Between 15 and 20 miles

Waiatarua Hills

Arthur Lydiard

Coach of 17 Olympic medalists

The basis of the "Lydiard system" was a 22-mile run over the Waiatarua range of hills on the west side of Auckland, New Zealand. Runners in Auckland know the loop as the "Waitaks." The hills rise from sea level to roughly 1,500 feet.

All the great Kiwi champions ran this loop, which started at Lydiard's house: Peter Snell, Murray Halberg, Barry McGee, John Davies, Dick Quax, Lorraine Moller. Lydiard mapped out the course back in the late 1950s, first running it alone as part of the 200-mile training weeks he did as an experiment on himself.

Lydiard says, "There are champions everywhere." He should know, because he found three of them—Snell, Halberg, and McGee—close to his Auckland home. Through trial and error, Lydiard discovered that 200 miles a week was too much, but he kept the Waiatarua 22-miler and it became the basis of his athletes' success.

"I believe in getting a good conditioning base," Lydiard said. "This is an undulating run, with no flat spots. The uphill running on it makes you strong, and being out for 22 miles increases your blood vascularization and your efficiency.

"It's old-fashioned to say it, but the fundamental physiological mechanics of running have not changed. We used to run 22 miles through the mountains and now you don't see people doing it much anymore. People have gotten soft and flabby. It's a question of application, not talking. Why did Peter (Snell) do the mileage and the 22-miler? Because he knew it made him a better runner. He saw the improvement."

Arthur Lydiard

Snell, now an exercise physiologist at the University of Texas Southwestern Medical Center, agrees. "That run was a good indicator for me. My best seasons correlated with how I did over the course. If I could maintain a hard 6-minute pace on it, I would have a terrific season afterward. It allowed me to do more of the intense interval training without burning out. I could do more of the volume of quality workouts coming off that background. That is what people don't understand now."

The first time Snell ran the Waiatarua Hills, he struggled in. Afterward, Lydiard said, "You know, Peter, when you get to the stage when you can run this hard and come back and do it again the following week and the next, you'll be right for training."

Snell did that and went on to upset world-record holder Roger Moens of Belgium in the 1960 Rome Olympic 800 meters. Four years later in Tokyo, Snell won both the 800- and 1,500-meter gold medals. "Arthur was absolutely right. I got into condition where I was in this tireless state and was able to do the training."

2 hours, 30 minutes over hills

Recovery	A continuous run
Pace	Solid
When to do	During base phase of training
Total distance	22 miles

The Cascade-Fourth Street Loop

Frank Shorter

Olympic marathon gold and silver medals

Pan American Games gold medalist (marathon, 10,000 meters)

Four-time Fukuoka marathon champion

U.S. national cross country champion (four times)

U.S. national and NCAA 6-mile champion

Shorter's long run was always two laps of a standard 10-mile loop, through a residential area with some rolling hills. Twenty miles or 2 hours, whichever came first. For Shorter, 20 miles usually did.

Shorter always had the mentality of a 5- and 10K track runner, even when he was winning the Olympic marathon. He kept his long runs just at 2 hours. Longer than that, he said, and he felt he was tearing his body down too much. Shorter found through the years that keeping his long runs at 2 hours on Sunday allowed him to recover in time for his Monday interval session.

The loop started at Cascade Avenue, went down Fourth Street, a road with a dearth of traffic that many runners use, then through campus and back to Cascade. Shorter ran this course twice, getting water when he passed by his house. The second loop was always faster than the first.

The two loops were always counted as 20 miles, but the exact distance was never measured. And even if the run was a bit less than 20 miles, Shorter emphasizes this key point: The exact distance on your long run does not matter, because you are doing the long run every week.

"Many runners take a buildup to a season, a 14-week marathon plan. I didn't have that buildup plan, but if you asked what I was doing the other 40 weeks of the year, I was running 20 miles every Sunday, every week."

Frank Shorter

Shorter did not rush into doing the long runs after winning the NCAA 6-mile title and graduating from Yale. "It took me a year of running with Jack Bacheler (in Gainesville with the Florida Track Club) to build up to 20 miles. Then I did it every Sunday for 10 years."

20 miles comprising two 10-mile loops

Recovery	A continuous run
Pace	Easy the first loop, picking it up the second
When to do	Once a week
Total distance	~20 miles

Woodhill Forest Long Run

Dick Quax
Former world-record holder, 5,000 meters
Silver medalist 1976 Olympic 5,000
Former coach, Athletics West

Fundamental to Quax's success were long runs between 2 and 3 hours at a pace fast enough to "apply constant pressure on both the central and the peripheral circulatory systems."

These runs were not Quax's favorites—those were running along a deserted beach and finishing with a plunge in the ocean, or running through a cool forest on a hot day. However, says Quax, "I judged workouts or training efforts on effectiveness rather than on what felt good."

And the most effective runs for Quax were the long runs that improved his aerobic capacity. The long, steady runs of over 2 hours built Quax's aerobic endurance, which he calls the building block for all successful distance running.

Quax and his training partners did their long runs in a number of places, the most popular being the Waiatarua hills (but less so as traffic has increased with Auckland's growth) and the Woodhill forest just outside of Auckland. It has numerous dirt roads, sand dunes, and miles of beach. In addition, Woodhill has some hilly sections and plenty of flat areas along the seashore. The runs at Woodhill always were over 2 hours, and often reached 2:45 and even just over 3 hours. That run was 30 miles. More typically, Quax's long run was 22 to 23 miles, and he would sometimes add another 5 to 6 miles in the evening.

As many as 10 runners—including former mile record holder, John Walker—would hook up and run the first 2 hours together, with the stronger runners pushing the pace over the last part of the workout. "Some days it would be all on right from the start and guys would be going for it, but that was pretty rare," says Quax.

These long runs started out "quite gentle," but would get as fast as 5:30 to 5:10 per mile by the end. Quax says his long runs always included hills because it made the run tougher and more interesting. However, it is not critical to include hills on your long runs, says Quax: "In Eugene we would run on the flat quite a bit and the results were still just as good."

According to Quax, during their long training, runners need to run "far enough and fast enough so that when they get into the final stages of a long run they have that 'heavy legs' feeling resulting from glycogen depletion. That is not a particularly satisfactory way of describing it but it's the best I know."

These long runs, as mentioned previously, increase the number of capillaries, which increases the blood supply to the muscles involved in running. The long run also "aids the recruitment of fast-twitch muscle fibers to do aerobic work, and it can be mentally relaxing."

Quax did most of his long runs during his 10- to 16-week base-building phase, but he continued running them until the start of his racing season, although he did not consider them as crucial then as when he was building his base. During double periodization—when he was racing in New Zealand and in Europe—Quax's base-building phase would be March through May for the northern hemisphere season and October through November for the southern hemisphere season.

"I found that when an athlete's racing form was in a bit of a decline, a couple of long runs would help a return to previous form or sometimes even better form. A good debate among your running mates might be to ask what is a long run. You'll be amazed at the answers you get!"

Dick Quax

And as for the deserted beach and cool forest runs? According to Quax, they are important as "a form of mental relaxation from the hard training that needs to be done on a daily basis."

A long 2- to 3-hour run

Recovery	A continuous run
Pace	Easy at the beginning, getting faster as the run progresses
When to do	During base-building phase of training, until racing begins
Total distance	Varies from 20 to 30 miles

Sandia Peak 18-Miler

David Morris

American marathon record holder, 2:09:30, and Eddy Hellybuck,
  winner of 19 marathons
PRs: 27:51 (10K), 1:00:49 (half-marathon) and 2:11:50 (marathon)

Morris and Hellybuck have a hilly 18-miler that gets progressively tougher as the run unfolds. The pair, who train together in Albuquerque, run three laps of a 6-mile trail in the foothills of Sandia Peak. The pair do the first 6 miles at a moderate pace of roughly 38 minutes; the second 6 miles are harder, and the third 6 miles are run in a fast 33 minutes. The altitude is 6,200 feet; water bottles are placed along the loop so the two can practice drinking fluids while running at a faster pace.

"This is our major test going into a big marathon or half-marathon. Six-minute miles seems easy, but it's not. It's a tough course, and we often see Khalid Khannouchi training on it as well. We did it together in 1998, when David won the Japanese Corporate Half in 1:02:00 and I won the Maui marathon in a 12-minute course record that same weekend. It has been an important workout ever since that time."

Eddy Hellybuck

Hellybuck said he and Morris like this run because the uphills and downhills, although not very steep, develop strength. There are "constant, constant rolling bunny hills, and the terrain is tricky there. It's a test of strength, and you get the long run in at the same time."

Three loops of a rolling 6-mile course

Recovery	A continuous run
Pace	Moderate at first, then getting progressively faster
When to do	Before a marathon or half-marathon
Total distance	18 miles

Treadmill Long Run

Kim Jones

2:26:40 marathoner
Former U.S. national marathon champion

Jones favors doing her long runs on a treadmill in her house. For the first hour she runs at a 7-minute pace. During the second hour, she keeps the same pace, but she raises the incline on the treadmill. First comes a segment at 8 percent, then 6, 4, 3, and 2 percent. Then the incline is raised back up in the same order. The run ends with 30 minutes of flat running at the same 7-minute pace.

"This workout is good because it teaches me how to change pace in the middle of a marathon. I don't watch TV when I'm doing it. It's too distracting and can make you fall off the treadmill. I do listen to music on headphones. My daughter made up a tape of music from the 1970s, '80s, and '90s. A little bit of everything."

Kim Jones

Long run on a treadmill

Recovery	A continuous run
Pace	7 minutes per mile
When to do	Once a week all year long
Total distance	21-1/2 miles

The Dudley Long Run

Mike Dudley

Winner Detroit (1996), Las Vegas (1994) marathons; 2nd Cal International
   marathon (1999)
PRs: 2:14.37 (marathon); 29:39.55 (10,000 meters); 48:57 (10 miles)

This long run is about 18 miles, followed by a 3- to 4-mile tempo run
at roughly 5-minute-mile pace at the end. Dudley has used this workout before each of his three fastest marathons.

"This comes at the end of a big week of over 120 miles. The workout
gives me confidence to run at or faster than marathon pace while
extremely tired. This is a strength workout I do two times during my
marathon buildup, once about 8 weeks out and the other time 4 weeks
out before a race."

Mike Dudley

Dudley's advice is to adjust the workout by running for about 1
hour, 50 minutes, in order to get your legs tired. Then throw on a 3-
to 4-mile tempo run at roughly your race pace for a half-marathon.
Finally, he adds, "I believe that health and consistency are the most
important items for the longer races."

A long run ending with a 3- to 4-mile tempo run

Recovery	A continuous run
Pace	Solid the first 18 miles, then at half-marathon race pace for the tempo run
When to do	Once a month for the two months leading up to a marathon
Total distance	21 to 22 miles

27-Mile Overdistance Run

Kathrine Switzer

Pioneer of women's running
TV commentator
Avon Running race director
PR: 2:51 (marathon)

Before her first marathon, Switzer ran an overdistance long run of 27 miles. Doing this gave Switzer a strong sense of confidence, a feeling she used in becoming the first woman to officially finish the Boston Marathon back in 1967. Switzer's long runs were done in the heavy snow and cold of Syracuse, New York.

Going beyond the marathon distance helped Switzer believe she could race the distance at a time when it was anathema for women to be running marathons. In fact, in 1967, Boston Marathon official Jock Semple tried to pull her off the course after spotting her during the race.

After doing the long runs during the winter, Switzer would add a track workout to her schedule, usually 20 quarters in about 80 seconds. Those were done on the track, alone, in the dark, because she was working full-time.

"Those were the two workouts that made the difference for me. The long run gave me confidence and the quarters improved my speed. It helped me to have training partners for these runs."

Kathrine Switzer

Switzer advises time-constrained runners to, first of all, do the long run at a pace you can finish the distance in. This will make you strong. Then, when you want to start racing, begin adding some speed to your training. "If you work out at 9-minute-mile pace, you'll race at 9-minute-mile pace," she says. "Some days you need to go faster."

An overdistance long run

Recovery	A continuous run
Pace	Whatever it takes to be able to complete the distance
When to do	During winter base phase
Total distance	27 miles

Hidden Hills 21-Miler (a Boston Simulation)

Benji Durden

1980 U.S. Olympic marathoner
3rd place Boston (1983)
Winner Nike and Houston Marathons
Coach of elite and non-elite runners
PR: 2:09:58 (marathon)

Durden finished his preparations for the Boston Marathon with a long run that started with a five-mile warm-up to the track at Stone Mountain High School in Georgia. The workout starts with a hard 1 kilometer, followed by a 200-meter jog. Then comes a hard 2 kilometers, followed by a 200-meter jog. Then another 1K with a 200-meter jog, then another 2K with a 200-meter jog. Then a 1K, a 200 jog, ending with a 2K. This is 10 kilometers of continuous running.

The segments within the workout add up in the following manner: 1,000 meters, 1,200, 3,200, 3,400, 4,400, 4,600, 6,600, 6,800, 7,800, 8,000, 10,000 meters. The final time for the whole 10K was 29:10. The 200s were run in about 50 seconds each, the kilometers in about 2:50, and the 2Ks in about 6:30.

Durden would then run an easy 15 minutes over to a hilly 5-mile measured course, where the Hidden Hills 5-mile road race is held. There, he ran a solid 25 minutes, wearing not just one sweatsuit, but two. The workout was completed with a 3-mile cool-down. Total distance was 21 miles, in about 2 hours, 10 minutes, including taking off and putting on sweats. Eleven days after this workout, Durden clocked 2:09:58 at Boston.

Durden chose this workout because it simulated the Boston Marathon, which is hilly in the middle of the course. This workout, as should be obvious, was a real confidence builder, because it showed Durden he was fit heading into the marathon. "It was the final icing on the cake" before backing off and starting his taper, Durden explained.

Boston Marathon Simulation

Recovery	200-meter jog between the 1Ks and 2Ks
Pace	2:50 (1Ks); 6:50 (2Ks), marathon race pace on the 5-mile segment
When to do	Last few weeks before a marathon
Total distance	21 miles, including alternating hard 1Ks and 2Ks on the track, totaling 10 kilometers, followed by a hard 5 miles over the hills

2

Chapter 2

Off-Road Training: Sparing Your Legs

Europeans often do their hard training on grass to decrease the stress on their legs. Running on a soft surface not only can save your legs and prevent injuries; it also makes the workouts more enjoyable. In addition, because these workouts are not as structured as those on the track, some runners say they do not have the mental stress of having to hit a certain time goal during an interval session.

Too much running on hard surfaces can make you susceptible to overuse injuries, those that occur in the knees, hips, and ankles. That is one reason grass running is popular in Europe. Another is that, until recently at least, tartan and all-weather tracks have been few and far between in Great Britain and other countries. It is not uncommon for Europeans to have to travel 30 miles, one way, to run on the track (which sometimes, as in New Zealand and Australia, are made of grass). That means runners are more apt to go to a park or field for their workouts.

It is different in the United States. Here, nearly every town with a high school has a track, and there are often several tracks in a runner's neighborhood to choose from. Why then should you do grass training? The reason is simple—these runs can give you a low-impact, yet still high-quality workout while strengthening your legs. And do not use the excuse that there is no grass to train on near your home or that finding grass is too inconvenient. You can always find a park with a strip of grass around the perimeter.

English runner Paul Davis-Hale was the first to point out to me the benefits of grass running. I recall going on a 10-mile run with Paul; I ran on the sidewalks while he ran across every lawn down the block. As soon as we passed a small park, he suggested we continue our run there. So we did, on the soft grass, going round and round for another hour while ducking beneath sprinklers.

The best runners, no matter what their countries of origin, have an innate sense of what they need to do and when to do it. Frank Shorter is a good example of this. He gravitated toward running on grass while preparing for his Olympic marathon gold medal. Shorter was fast enough to set the U.S. 10,000-meter record in the qualifying round of the Munich Olympic Games, then break the record in the final, where he clocked 27:49 to finish fifth, behind Lasse Viren.

Yet one of Shorter's favorite workouts while preparing for the Olympics was not on the track or the roads, but on a rough grass field about 500 meters around. Intramural flag football games would be going on in the center of the field while Shorter and his training partners did their workouts along its outer edge, dodging Frisbees and footballs.

It is unfortunate that there is not a big cross country season in the United States, because that would, perhaps, increase the popularity of grass running. Cross country running in Europe, as some of you might know, is a different animal than its cousin in the United States. European-style cross country is done over hills and through tall grass and mud. U.S. cross country runners often race on manicured golf courses, or even on roads part of the way! If we had real mud-and-guts cross country, perhaps we would be more apt to go out and train on the grass.

Running over grass will feel awkward at first. The uneven, thicker surface will feel a bit like running through snow. However, if you make grass running a part of your regular training regime, you will soon learn to increase your knee lift and get more pushoff with each stride, while likely decreasing the risk of injury. As I will continually mention in this book, longevity is the key to success in long-distance running, no matter what your level or your goal. And what will increase the longevity of your running? Making your training enjoyable, which grass running in a nice setting can do.

On your next run, try a little experiment. Jog over to your local park and run some strides on a concrete sidewalk. Then run some strides on the grass. Feel the difference? Now multiply that by several years and hundreds or even thousands of miles. Imagine the different stress levels your legs experience on each surface.

It is easy to put some European-style grass running into your training regime. These runs can be done any time of the year, both as recovery runs and as hard sessions (if you are training for a track race, of course, you will need to spend time on the track doing interval sessions). Running speedwork on the grass means you can often avoid the curves found on the track, and it will help you develop a sense of pace.

Head over to the best grass park you can find, and run your workout by time, not distance. Try it; like the Europeans, you might just find that it adds freshness to both your training and your legs.

Shorter's Grass Repeats

Frank Shorter was the first runner to bring track speed and a track runner's mentality to the marathon. He surprised world-record holder Derek Clayton and Ron Hill, then the second fastest marathoner ever, in the 1972 Munich Olympic marathon with an early surge that gave him a lead he held to the end.

The basis for that gold-medal-winning surge can be found during Shorter's several years of training on the grass of Franklin Field on the University of Colorado campus. Before the field was paved over so a new mathematics building could be built, it was the scene of many fast workouts by Shorter, members of the Colorado Track Club, and the university track and cross country teams. After Shorter was termed "The Man Who Invented Running" on a magazine cover, one journalist actually called the field, only somewhat lightheartedly, "the field where running began," because Shorter did so many workouts there.

Shorter was able to excel at cross country and track and on the roads in part because he ran intervals all year long. Running on the grass, he says, allowed him to do that, because it reduced the stress resulting from his fast running. Shorter never varied from his set routine when getting ready for his grass workouts. He lived up on Lincoln Place near the base of Flagstaff Mountain, about 2 miles from campus. He would warm up from his house, going down Cascade Avenue and beneath Broadway, then loop through campus. He would pass Old Main and Macky Auditorium and run across the bridge over Varsity Pond before ending up at the field, across from the football stadium and next to the Physics building.

The workout was a ladder. First came three laps around the field, followed by a lap-and-a-half jog. Next was two laps hard, with one lap recovery. Then came three to six half-laps, with a straightaway recovery in between.

Shorter says he liked these workouts because they saved his legs. He did not worry about how fast he was passing the 400- or 800-meter marks, or even exactly where the 400 and 800 splits were. He explains it this way: "If I wanted to run real fast I went on the track; if I felt I needed to back off I went on the grass. The perceived effort was 65 percent. Running on the grass is how I backed off from my intervals."

A footnote: Because of the snow and cold in the winter months, it is not possible to run on grass all year long in Colorado. That was an unfortunate climatic fact for Shorter. In 1976, he was fitter than he was before the 1972 Olympics. He would have, some say, run much faster over 10,000 meters than he had in the previous Olympics. But Shorter broke a bone in his foot while running intervals on the indoor track in the winter of 1976. He even remembers the exact date, February 23. Shorter kept training, but the injury forced him to skip the 10,000-meters at the Olympics. As it turned out, the 10,000 final was not a deep affair. Lasse Viren sat behind Carlos Lopes before running in for the win. And if Shorter had been able to run on the grass instead of the track that winter? "Without a broken foot, I'm certain Frank would have had a medal in the 10,000," said Pablo Vigil, an elite runner training with Shorter at the time. "He was in great shape."

3 laps, 2 laps, I lap, and 3 to 6 half-lap repeats around a grass field

Recovery	Half the distance
Pace	65% perceived effort
When to do	Year round, if conditions allow for it
Total distance	Roughly 3 miles of hard running

10 x I lap on a grass field

Recovery	Half-lap jog
Pace	65% perceived effort
When to do	Year round, if conditions allow for it
Total distance	Roughly 3 miles of hard running

Royal Air Force Repeats

Steve Jones

Former world-record holder for marathon

Former world-record holder for half-marathon

PRs: 2:07:13 (marathon); 60:59 (half-marathon); 27:39 (10K)

One of Jones's favorite workouts was 4×5 minutes hard on a grass field at the RAF St. Athan Air Force base, with a 2-minute recovery between each hard segment. The repeats were a timed workout, but they were not run over a set distance. Jones had several other standard workouts on the grass, such as 14×2 minutes or 8×3 minutes, with 90 seconds recovery, and 16×1 minute with a minute recovery.

Before he turned to the marathon, Jones ran fast enough on the track to make the British Olympic team in the 10,000-meters, placing eighth in the 1984 Olympics. During the winter and spring before he ran his best track times of 13:18 and 27:38, Jones rarely set foot on a track. Instead, he would do his workouts on the grass. That meant his legs were fresher and he was fitter when he began track intervals during the summer. In addition, Jones would run in his local club races, sometimes three or four times a week, as a way to gauge his training.

"For many years little of my work was done on the track, even though I was racing on the track and did some workouts on the track. It was just much more beneficial for me not to have the stress of trying to run 60-second quarters, or 2:08s or 2:06s (for 800 meters), even though I was probably running that pace in this workout. It wasn't a measured distance; what was measured was the time. I was squeezing 60 seconds into a minute."

Steve Jones

In these grass workouts, as opposed to a fartlek session, there were no markers or points of reference to run to; "I just ran to my watch," Jones explained. "I would set my watch and start when it beeped, then stop when it beeped again."

Running many of his quality sessions on the grass allowed Jones to do a significant amount of running near his threshold. That is mentally difficult to do, but Jones was tough enough to push himself that way in training. The softness of the grass helped keep him injury free. This kind of training allowed Jones to do the years of threshold running that resulted in his epic front-running marathon at Chicago in 1985. During that marathon, Jones passed halfway in 1:01, not far off the then half-marathon world record.

4 x 5 minutes on a grass field with a 2-minute recovery between each hard effort

Pace	A hard effort
When to do	Fall, winter, or spring
Total distance	Varies on your pace
Variations	14 × 2 minutes with 90 seconds recovery, or 16 × 1 minute with a 30-second recovery

Colleen and Bobby McGee

Colleen De Reuck

Three-time Olympian in the marathon and 10,000-meters
World road record holder for 10 miles (51:16)
World road record holder for 20K (1:05:11)

This workout was designed by De Reuck's coach, Bobby McGee. He uses it to help his runners make the transition from winter training to track work. The session is 3 × 3-minute surges, with what De Reuck calls a "3,000-meter mindset." She thinks of this part of the workout as running 3 × 1,000-meter pickups, with a 90-second recovery jog between each one.

This set is followed by a 3-minute recovery jog. Next come 4 × 30-second bursts with an 800-meter mindset, with an easy 1-minute jog between each burst. After another 3-minute recovery jog, De Reuck runs 3 × 5 minutes with a 2-minute recovery jog between each hard effort. In this part of the workout, she has the mindset of a 5,000-meter runner. Finally, after another 3-minute recovery come 4 × 1 minute at 1,500-meter or mile race effort, with a 1-minute recovery jog between each.

The key to this workout, according to De Reuck, is running it on grass or trails, or even sand. "Try to husband your resources so as to give a concerted effort throughout," she says.

Another key for De Reuck is that she does not spend her day worrying about her next workout. She urges those of you wanting to become good runners to maintain a balance between your running and your life. Have other priorities besides your training and "see beyond your next race."

"When you race or train, concentrate 100 percent on what you are doing—be a runner. But when it's over, be fully all the other things you are in your life—partner, parent, professional, friend, worker, hobbyist, etc." In the end, if you enjoy your running then all else will fall into place."

Colleen De Reuck

Bursts and surges of varying lengths

Recovery	90-second jog between 3 × 3 minute surges with 3-minute jog between sets. 2-minute recovery between 3 × 5-minute repeats and 1-minute recovery between the hard 4 × 1-minutes
Pace	Solid, but not all out
When to do	In the spring, after base phase of training
Total distance	10 to 12 miles, including warm-up and cool-down

Montana Cone to Cone

Shannon Butler

1991 NCAA 10,000-meter champion
1992 U.S. national 10,000-meter champion
1992 World Cross Country trials winner
PRs: 27:59 (10K); 13:33 (5K)

After a summer spent fishing and hunting in the Montana mountains, Butler was able to get fit quickly in part because of a workout consisting of 20 × 60-second runs diagonally across a grass field with a short recovery. Cones were set up at the corners of a field on the campus of Montana State University, roughly a quarter-mile apart. Butler would run from cone to cone, then jog before starting the next repeat.

This workout was done each week during the fall. At the beginning of the season, Butler and his teammates would take a minute rest between each repeat. Every 2 weeks the recovery was dropped down a bit. Variations of this workout included 45-second repeats, and even shorter as a championship race neared.

"We did this on a small grass field, the only one on campus. There were no turns during the workout, and with the short recovery you were always anaerobic; you could get in shape so fast. Each week we would get better and better at the workout. It was great because we would wear spikes and be ready for our races. This workout really helped me when I was second at NCAA cross country. It got my legs and feet feeling different."

Shannon Butler

This grass workout, Butler adds, was important because it strengthened the tendons and ligaments in his lower legs while at the same time stretching out his Achilles tendons. "The support structure of your lower legs, all the little muscles and tendons of your lower feet, get stronger in this workout in a way they don't when you run on the roads."

In addition, Butler ran on the field every morning while in college because he was prone to injuries and the soft surface made his legs feel better. He liked it so much that he even ran around the field in the winter.

20 x 60 seconds on the grass

Recovery	One minute or less
Pace	Hard
When to do	When preparing for cross country season
Total distance	10 miles

Carr's Cross Country Simulation

Donna Garcia

Two-time World Cross Country team member
Made the team in both the 4K and 8K in 2000
PRs: 32:39 (10,000 meters); 15:57.13 (5,000 meters)

One of Garcia's standard workouts is mile repeats on a cross country course at the Al Bishop complex in Marietta, Georgia. The facility hosted the Georgia high school cross country championships for several years.

The course is a 1-mile loop starting on a grass straightaway. The route crosses a creek over a dirt bridge and then crosses another field. The course then goes on to gravel for a bit before heading uphill on the red clay. It climbs until roughly the 1,000-meter mark; it then turns down and enters some woods. The route continues on dirt down through the woods before emptying out about 100 meters on the grass straightaway from the spot where the loop starts.

"The workout Donna often does here is three to four repeats with an emphasis on a quick start, settling in, maintaining during the uphill section, keeping composure through the woods and downhill, with a gradual increase of turnover on the last straightaway."

Andy Carr, Garcia's coach

Donna began these repeats 3 years ago at around 5:30 for a loop. She has gradually dropped that to around 5:15 per loop. These workouts usually go with at least a 20-minute warm-up and at least a 20-minute cool-down.

Carr says doing workouts over a varied loop can be helpful for any runner, especially when the courses are varied enough not to become boring. The course at the Al Bishop center is a softball complex with many trails and paths, as well as a permanent cross country finishing area. "Donna and I both feel this is the workout that simulates cross country racing, terrain, and competitive feel. It's been the backbone for her hard workouts and success in her cross country racing. It's great because very few people come to train there, it's all off-road and contains grass, trails, ups and downs, and long straightaways."

Garcia never runs on the track during the cross country season. She does another workout on a similar loop at the Marist School in North Atlanta. It is roughly a 1-1/2-mile loop with some long grass straightaways. In addition, this loop has some bark-chip trails with very short, steep hills. For a workout here, Garcia runs 2 to 4 repeats with about 5 minutes recovery between each repeat. Carr changes the rest based on Garcia's mileage and race schedule. Running her workouts on the grass and trails reduces the risk of injuries from overuse or too much pounding, Carr says. It is also "refreshing for runners, since they don't have to deal with traffic and can go on a trail that's very well groomed."

3 to 4 x 1 mile cross country repeats on grass, gravel, and clay

Pace	10K-race pace
Recovery	5 minutes between repeats; a 20-minute warm-up and 20-minute cool-down
When to do	Cross country season
Total distance	10 miles, with warm-up and cool-down

The Rock Creek 10-Miler

Deena Drossin

American record holder for 5K on the road (15:06)
Four-time national cross country champion
2000 U.S. cross country champion, 4K and 8K
Six-time IAAF World Cross Country competitor
Eight-time All-American at University of Arkansas
2000 Olympic trials 10,000 meter winner

Drossin's favorite workout is a 10-mile uphill run following Rock Creek in the San Juan mountains of southwestern Colorado. It starts at 7,500 feet altitude and ends at treeline.

The run is tough, but fun. Coach Joe Vigil drives Drossin and some of his good male runners to the start of the run, about 30 minutes from Alamosa. Drossin starts before the men, getting roughly a mile head start. The men then try to catch her. The run is on a dirt road, past campsites and good hunting and fishing sites, which makes it more pleasant.

"This is a very beautiful run we usually do in the fall. It certainly is a challenging run where the air is thin. There is no flat part on it. What I like is that it's an intense workout, but there's a lot of camaraderie on the run."

Deena Drossin

Drossin makes the run more interesting by often looking over her shoulder, surging and seeing if the men are catching her. As the fickle mountain temperature changes during the run, Drossin takes off or puts on clothing. Vigil has doughnuts or bananas waiting for the runners at the top as their reward.

"We do this run for strength. We don't run for time; we go for however long it takes. This workout helps your cardiovascular endurance and is a good key workout."

Coach Vigil

Uphill dirt-road run

Recovery	No break in the run
Pace	Solid
When to do	Fall
Total distance	10 miles

Alamosa Miles

Joe Vigil

PhD in sports physiology

Coach of numerous elite athletes, including Deena Drossin and Pat Porter (9 U.S. cross country titles)

Coach of 425 All-Americans and 89 national champions during his 28 years at Adams State University

Every Thursday since the mid-1960s, all of Vigil's athletes have run mile repeats, with a 3-minute jog recovery, around Cole Park in Alamosa, Colorado. Elite runners, ranging in the past from Pat Porter to Juma Ikangga and Gelindo Bordin, to current elites such as Deena Drossin and Peter de la Cerda, have been doing this workout. The number of repeats varies from five at the beginning of the season to one or two leading up to a big competition in the racing season.

Vigil calls these mile repeats his "bread-and-butter workout." It is the one workout in a given year that starts his runners on their progression. "It doesn't matter if you are a 5,000-meter runner, a 10,000-meter runner, or a marathoner; you have the pace you want to run toward a specific goal, and you get there by percentages. It's fun to see the runners progress as the season goes on.

"For example, a 5K guy who wants to run 13:30 will start off toward 4:20 (per mile) by six. As they adapt, the runners get stronger, and that's fun. The pace we start running our mile repeats all depends on the runners, on how much base they got in during the off-season.

"This is what's called a *lactate tolerance* workout, so the anaerobic threshold level goes up and the time for the miles goes down. It works because a 3- to 6-minute effort is the workout in which endurance is built. We use this workout for many different reasons."

Joe Vigil

One reason is that 3 to 6 minutes of running lets the runners stay together. You get fatigued, but you can hang on to the end. The best times have been between 4:15 and 4:18 per mile. We don't start off at that speed. Deena (Drossin) has been the fastest of the women. It's amazing that she can do 4 times 4:45 at altitude."

Vigil's athletes also run 400-meter repeats on the track. "The times on these intervals depend on a runner's ability to maintain the pace he or she asks each to shoot for. For example, a runner with a goal of 27:50 (for 10K) will run 67 to 68 seconds a quarter. Drossin will run hers in 70 to 71 seconds."

According to Vigil, the mile repeat workout can be helpful for anyone. The principle is the same for all kinds of runners; only the intensity is different. "I can't remember when I started doing this workout, maybe 20 to 25 years ago. You try different things over the years, and this one worked. It's just like a heart patient, who as he exercises his heart begins increasing the intensity."

Vigil says his runners do the miles at Cole Park instead of on the track "for a change of scenery."

"We do these milers once a week, all year long. We start with five of them at a slower pace in the beginning of the year, during our base training, after we've taken a few weeks off after the track season. This is the workout we all base our fitness off of. At the beginning of the year I run them in 5 minutes to 5:05. Before a race we'll do one or two of them as fast as we can. (Before the 2000 IAAF World Cross Country Championships, Drossin ran two all-out miles in 4:42). A lot of legs have been running around the trail."

"Absolutely it helps me running with the group of guys. I feel it has made me a more aggressive runner. I try to stay with the guys for as long as I can. I know I will never win, but I keep on trying."

Deena Drossin

Mile repeats around a park

Recovery	3-minute jog
Pace	Varies, depending on the number and the time of year
When to do	All year long
Total distance	11 miles

Race Pace Mile Repeats

Steve Plasencia

Head cross country coach, University of Minnesota

Two-time Olympian, personal bests of 13:19.37 (5K), 27:45.20 (10K), 2:12.51 (marathon)

American masters record holder 3,000 meters (8:24), 5K, 15K (45:10), half-marathon (1:05:40), 25K (1:18:38).

During his long career, Plasencia has consistently run 6 × mile at his 10K race pace. Plasencia takes a 400-meter recovery jog, in about 2-1/2 minutes, in between each mile.

Plasencia says this is the one workout over the years that tells him what kind of shape he is in for 10,000 meters. He typically does it on the track. When he lived and trained in Eugene, he would run it on the Oregon Adidas trail, a woodchip mile loop marked every 100 meters.

According to Plasencia, "when you start out on the first mile you are not focusing that hard, but it climbs on you as the workout goes on. By numbers 4 and 5 in particular, your quads are aching."

Plasencia's general rule of thumb is that if he could average a certain pace for the 6 miles, he would be able to run that pace for a 10,000-meter race. For example, if he averaged 4:30 per mile, he could run 28 minutes. "I like this workout because it gave me a pretty direct indicator of where I stood."

This workout was usually run alone, meaning that Plasencia did not have the advantage of people pulling him along.

> "You would think that 6 separate miles would not be equivalent to 10K, but if you can do it by yourself and hold up during the workout it is a pretty good indicator of your 10K time."
>
> Steve Plasencia

For runners not at his level, Plasencia does not recommend doing 6 × 1 mile. "The volume will be less, because it is a pretty heavy-duty interval workout. I was running 100 miles a week when I would do this workout." Someone aiming for a 40-minute 10K would do four times a mile at roughly 6:10 per mile. "You could do more, but if you are not doing the volume (of mileage) you could be beat up from the workout."

Always keep the miles at your target 10K-race pace, Plasencia recommends.

"If you find that difficult and start slowing down, cut back on the number of miles you are doing to keep the miles at your race pace."

6 x mile

Recovery	400-meter jog in 2-1/2 minutes
Pace	10K-race pace per mile. For example, a 34-minute 10K runner would do the miles in 5:30; a 36-minute 10K runner in roughly 5:54 per mile, and a 40-minute 10K runner in 6:10.
Total distance	10 miles

Lawson's Race Tempo Workout

Jerry Lawson

Former American record holder in the marathon, 2:09:35
Cal International Marathon winner (2:10:27)

This is a workout that can be done on the track, or off-road if the distance is measured. Lawson would run it when he was attending Boston University and getting ready for the Penn Relays.

After a 3-mile warm-up, this workout starts off with 1-1/2 miles in 6:43, followed by a 3-minute recovery. Then comes 1-1/4 miles in 5:37, with another 3-minute recovery. Next is 1 mile in 4:30, again with a 3-minute recovery. Then comes 1,200 meters in 3:21, with a 6-minute recovery before finishing with a 2-mile in 9:08. The session ends with a 3-mile cool-down.

When Lawson runs this he will have some training partners run part of the repeats with him. In 1993, this was his first workout of the year, and when Lawson "nailed it," it set the tone for the rest of his season. He says his coach at Boston University, Bruce Lehane, had Lawson do this workout to learn to run race tempo under control. That is the purpose of the hard 2-miles to finish off the workout.

"When I can hit this workout I KNOW I'm in such solid shape that there is little I can't do. This is one of the first 'real' workouts I run when getting ready for the Olympic trials."

Jerry Lawson

Lawson says that while this might be too advanced a workout for some runners, it can be adjusted to good effect after several weeks of workouts. After a warm-up, run 10 minutes hard, then 3 minutes easy. Then 8 minutes hard, 3 minutes easy; next 6 minutes hard, 3 minutes easy; followed by 4 minutes hard, 6 minutes easy. If you are strong enough, go another 10 minutes hard, end the workout, then finish up with a 10-15 minute cool-down.

This is a way to simulate Lawson's workout without the stress of having to hit specific times.

Race Tempo Efforts

Recovery
3 minutes between each of the segments consisting of 1-1/4 miles in 5:37; 1 mile in 4:30; 1,200 m in 3:21; 2 miles in 9:08 6 minutes are taken before the final 2 miles

Pace
Faster than your target race pace

Emil's 100 x 400 meters

Emil Zatopek

18 world records
Only man to win Olympic marathon, 10,000 and 5,000-meter gold medals (1952)
1948 Olympic gold medal 10,000 meters, silver 5,000 meters

"Why should I practice running slow?" Emil Zatopek asked as a young runner in Prague. "I already know how to run slow. I must learn how to run fast."

Zatopek is one of the most beloved runners ever, both for his training innovations and his iron will, as well as for his humanistic, international approach to running and to life. He questioned the training methods of his day and formulated his own ideas. The basis of his revolutionary training was combining speed and stamina in the same workout.

"Speed, by running short distance, maybe 100 meters, and stamina, not to have rest during the training. 100 meters fast, and 100 meters easy. This way I was able to run faster than by using the former training methods."

Emil Zatopek

When told by his clubmates that he was not a sprinter, Zatopek replied, "If I run 100 meters 30 times, that is 3 kilometers and no longer a sprint."

In 1954, Zatopek broke the 5,000-meter world record, which had stood for 12 years, by running 13:57.2. The next day he became the first runner to break the 29-minute barrier in the 10K, clocking 28:54.2. In order to prepare for those records Zatopek did the toughest training of his life, out in a pine forest near his favorite track in Houtska Stadium, set in a pine forest near Prague: 100 × 400 meters; 50 times in the morning, 50 times in the afternoon, with a 150-meter recovery. "Every day for 2 weeks. Oh, it was a lot of work," he said. "I was able to change this quantity of training into quality of running."

100 x 400 meters

Recovery	150-meter jog
Pace	Hard but not so fast that you can't finish the 400s
Distance	30 miles

Plaatjes' Marathon Indicator

Mark Plaatjes

Gold medal, World Championship marathon (1993)
Winner, 30 marathons
Coach of Scotty Larson (4th, 2000 Olympic trials marathon)
PR: 2:08:50

Three weeks before all of his marathons, Plaatjes always ran a workout of 10 × 1 mile, with a minute recovery, at the pace he planned on maintaining during his marathon. The best he ever ran the workout was leading up to the Stuttegart World Championships. During a training stint in Holland, Plaatjes averaged 4:48 per mile, before going on to win the gold medal.

Plaatjes typically ran this workout on the track but says most runners are better off doing it on the roads or grass if they have a mile marked off. Ten mile repeats might sound like a lot, but Plaatjes believes anyone planning on running a marathon should be able to do this session.

"It gives you a final idea of what you can run in the marathon. If you think about it, it is simple: If you can't run 10 times a mile at your anticipated pace, you can't go and run 26 times a mile in the marathon. This should be a real good indicator for you."

Mark Plaatjes

Runners should not be completely trashed after finishing this workout. "I was very, very comfortable doing this," Plaatjes says. "You should be able to finish and say, 'Oh, I could carry on.'" After completing this workout, Plaatjes would then top off his marathon preparation with a couple of Rob de Castella 8 × 400 meter sessions (chapter 4) and a final long run 10 days before his race. He would rest for the five days leading up to his marathon.

10 x 1 Mile

Recovery	1 minute between each mile
Pace	Anticipated marathon race pace
When to do	Three weeks before marathon

Radcliffe's Off-Road 2K Reps

Paula Radcliffe

Great Britain Female Athlete of the Year (1999)
3-time World Cross Country medalist
World Championship 10,000 meters silver medal
World Junior Cross Country champion
World road record, 5 miles (24:54)
World road record, 8K (24:38)

Paula Radcliffe is a world-class competitior on the track and roads as well as in cross country. She has two important workouts, one off-road, the other on the track. The first is 5 × 6 minute, 30-second efforts, with a 90-second recovery. This session is meant to simulate 5 × 2,000 meter reps (which adds up to 10K), although Radcliffe would likely be running more than 2K on each rep if the distance was measured. The pace is faster than 5-minutes per mile.

The key to the workout, which is done every week after her base phase of training, is that the 90-second jog means Radcliffe is barely recovering before starting the next hard effort. During her altitude training, this makes the workout even more difficult.

Radcliffe's track session, done once every couple of weeks, comprises various distances, starting with 2,000 meters and going down to 400 meters. The speed of each effort increases as the distance decreases. The recovery is the same 90 seconds (2 minutes at altitude).

Radcliffe likes these workouts because "they are hard and feel as though they must do some good." She also says the track session is more interesting than standard repetitions.

"Regular runners can modify the workout to suit them by changing speeds and starting with fewer reps and building up gradually. They should also start with longer recoveries and decrease them in time."

Paula Radcliffe

It took Radcliffe years of steady progression from the junior ranks to be able to handle this kind of work. She urges those wanting to get faster not to jump into these sessions too soon.

5 x 6 minute, 30-second reps

Recovery	90 seconds
Pace Hard	(Sub-5 minute miles for Radcliffe)
When to do	During entire racing season

Chapter 3

Fartlek Training: Mixing It Up

A long time ago, far away in the woods and fields of Sweden, Gunder Hägg and Arne Anderson ran workouts called *fartlek* on their way to becoming the top two milers in the world. The term comes from a Swedish word usually translated as "speedplay." Fartlek was popularized by the pair of milers, who knocked loudly on the door of the 4-minute mile in the 1940s.

Let's be honest about something: training is often difficult, seemingly unending work. Just as Sisyphus is doomed to forever push his heavy rock up a steep mountainside, so does it seem that a runner's fate is ceaseless sweat and labor, toil and training. Finish one great workout or long run, and you know in the back of your mind that another is waiting patiently for you later in the week.

The only way to keep your training going consistently, year after year, is to make it fun whenever possible, even while doing a tough workout. Fartlek helps you do that by keeping an element of play in the workout without reducing your hard running.

Remember when you were a kid, playing in your schoolyard on one of these long, magical summer evenings that lingered on and on? Maybe you played "kick the can." Or perhaps you and your friends were out there chasing each other across one of those freshly mowed grass fields, playing tag. You would sprint, then rest, then sprint again, looking over your shoulder and laughing a rib-busting, out-of-breath laugh as you tried to stay a step ahead of your friends. How fun running was then, how enjoyable. It was not work; it was a simple and pure pleasure.

That kind of joyful play in running we all experienced as children can be recaptured in a fartlek session. Simply put, fartlek is unstructured fast running over a variety of terrain, interspersed with recovery running.

How far or fast should you run on the hard segments? That's the great thing about fartlek—it is all up to you. There is no coach with a stopwatch telling you when to start and stop, no lines on the track to stay within, no miles to repeat or meters to sprint. Pick out a lovely pine tree atop a hill, and run hard to the tree, or to a fence, bush, or whatever strikes your fancy.

During fartlek, you might be running along when all at once you or your training partner take off, for no apparent reason. Run fast simply because you feel like it, and stop when you feel it is time. Take a short recovery sometimes, other times take a long recovery before the next hard effort.

How many hard segments should you run, how many total miles, how much warm-up and cool-down? Who knows? Who cares? Save that for another day, another run. This is fartlek: Run hard for as long as you want, just because you feel like it. You will get an excellent workout in without the mental pressures you sometimes have on the track.

Fartlek can take us back beyond our childhoods, back to the primal origins of running, as I discovered on a trip to Kenya. When I was in the Rift Valley training with the young runners, we would sometimes run across pathless fields, the sun hanging low above the Rift Valley escarpment in the distance. I remember thinking, This is how our ancestors must have run when they first stood up on two legs not so far from here.

Maybe those first runners chased antelope or wildebeest to get food, or maybe they were chased by lions or leopards who hoped to make them food. Either way, when they were done chasing or being chased through the valley, I have the feeling that our first ancestors—call them Adam and Eve if you like—would then run for the sheer joy of it, simply because they felt like it. Just as we should sometimes.

Fartlek is less structured than track workouts or repeats on the road, which is just the point: We runners, especially competitive runners, too often are ruled by the clock. During a fartlek workout, run as you were meant to run, with no thought of split times, kilometers, lactate threshold, or your maximum heart rate.

As you continue doing fartlek, you will learn to run with the landscape; often natural stopping and starting points for the hard running will appear in the contours of the land. You might run hard up a hill and jog down the other side. Or you might sprint through a clearing until you reach the edge of the woods. If the trail disappears around a curve in front of you, run to the curve, recover until you get to the next curve, and then sprint again.

Where can you run a fartlek workout? True fartlek training should be done out away from town, says Bruce Gomez, track coach at Taos (New Mexico) High School. But any park will do, or even streets if nothing else is available. Give no thought to time or distance, or how many hard efforts you are putting in. Just run hard because you feel like running hard, sometimes longer, sometimes shorter. Mix it up and try to beat your training partner to the next tree or bridge. Run all out, run gently, run steady, run slowly, run strong, run uphill, run downhill, all in the same workout. "Most of all, run free," says Gomez.

And try this the next time you have a workout scheduled: Take off your watch and toss it on the floor. Kick it beneath your bed or throw it in a drawer. Close the drawer, go out the door and start running, just you, your shoes, and the landscape. Not only will running fartlek add longevity to your legs if you do it on a soft surface; running this workout with zest and élan in the true spirit of running can also add years to your mental health.

The "Mono" Fartlek Workout

Shaun Creighton

Australian record holder 10,000 meters, 27:31
2000 Olympic runner in 10,000 meters
PRs: 2:10:22 (marathon); 3:55 (mile)

One of Shaun Creighton's main speed workouts before breaking Ron Clarke's long-standing Australian 10,000-meter record was the *mono-fartlek,* named for marathoner Steve Moneghetti. The mono is essentially 20 minutes of fartlek with a fast recovery. The recovery time is the same time as the fast efforts.

The workout starts with a 6-kilometer jog to Lake Ginnendera, out past the National Institute of Sports on the outskirts of Canberra, Australia. The workout consists of 2 × 90 seconds with a 90-second float, 4 × 60 seconds with a 60-second float, 4 × 30 seconds fast, with 30-second floats, and finally 4 × 15 seconds on, 15 seconds off.

Creighton favors this workout in part because he likes workouts that add up to 20 minutes. "If I do 40 minutes it wipes me out, and 10 minutes is not enough. The whole thing sounds easier on paper than it is," says Creighton. "By the time you get to 15 seconds you are not sprinting; you are just hanging on and working hard."

Creighton has great track credentials, having run 3:38 for 1,500 meters, 7:41 for 3,000, 8:16 for steeplechase, and 13:17 for 5,000 meters in addition to his 27:31 Australian record. Interestingly enough, despite these fast track times Creighton does not work out much on the track. In fact, in 1997 he dug himself into a deep hole by doing too much intense track work.

"I saw all the guys running 13 minutes (for 5K) and decided to change my training," said Creighton. He got so tired that he ran more than 14 minutes for 5K at a big track meet in Europe. He had to cancel his European season and return home for a rest. After taking two weeks completely off, Creighton rebounded to run 2:10 at Berlin. That winter, he started a buildup for a spring marathon. During the next 8 months, he ran just two track workouts. Yet in the spring he easily won the Australian 5,000-meter title in 13:24. His main workout during those 8 months? The monofartlek. Here is why the session works:

"Unlike an ordinary tempo run, with this your legs can get used to the change of pace. I'm not a big one for getting on the track all the time. In the monofartlek, you run how you feel and can get in the training without the scrutiny of the clock. If you are a bit tired, you can get the same training effort in but not be worried about the time. It is the effort that matters, not the precise time."

Shaun Creighton

This workout is a regular part of Creighton's training. He has noticed over the years that his pulse during the recovery after the 15 and 30 seconds is higher than the effort in the 90 seconds. "By keeping the float hard, your pulse does not get down," he explains. "It makes it quite hard."

"And here is an interesting fact," he adds. "I often do this workout in Canberra near where I live. The lake is 7K around, just perfect for this workout. If I run it really well, I will get in a full lap. The 10 farthest distances I have gone have been with the fartlek workout and not a pure tempo run, which I also do sometimes."

The reason he runs farther during the monofartlek than on the tempo run, Creighton says, is that he is going a lot faster on the reps. But when he floats during the monofartlek, he is still going quite steady. "So really, the average velocity works out to be a bit faster."

Creighton picked up the workout from Moneghetti, who does the same session around a 6K lake near his home in Bellaroot, Australia. This workout is a way to get in quite a bit of speed without going on a track. If Creighton is training for the track more than the marathon, he uses a flat section to run his reps, and slows down the float a little. That way it is a lactic acid workout, what Creighton calls a "speed fartlek session. What I do is sprint like hell in the reps."

To make the workout efficient, Creighton uses a watch with a beeper set to go off every 30 seconds to keep track of when to start the next hard effort. That, however, is not required during this workout.

(continued)

The "Mono" Fartlek Workout (continued)

20 minutes of fartlek with fast recovery

Recovery   Same amount of time as the hard efforts (The session starts off with 2 × 90 seconds with a 90-second float, followed by 4 × 60 seconds with a 60-second float, 4 × 30 seconds with a 30-second float, and finally 4 × 15 seconds with a 15-second float.)

Pace   Fast on the hard efforts, a float on the recovery

When to do   All year long

Total distance   10 miles

LeMay's 10-Mile Icebreaker

Joe LeMay

2nd 1996 Olympic trials 10,000 meters
Three-time Olympic marathon trials qualifier
U.S. 20K champion in 1995-96; 15K champ, 1997
PRs: 28:00 (10K), 2:14:58 (marathon)

In the middle of a 10-mile run, LeMay runs six sets of 3 minutes hard/ 2 minutes easy. That way, he is starting a hard effort every 5 minutes. The 10-miler starts and finishes with roughly 15 minutes of easy running. This is what LeMay calls an "ice-breaker" workout, a good one to do if you have not done any speedwork for a while.

LeMay works full-time and has to fit his 100-mile weeks in around a busy schedule. He does not often have time to go to the track for an interval session, so he will do this fartlek while on a 10-mile run.

> "I like this workout because I don't have to go to the track to do it. It actually saves me time by speeding up what would otherwise be just a regular run."
>
> Joe LeMay

If you are pressed for time, LeMay recommends reducing the warm-up and warm-down to 10 minutes. "You can do it almost any time, and under a variety of conditions," he says. As the year progresses, LeMay will begin going to the track for speedwork.

Six hard 3-minute efforts

Recovery	2 minutes
Pace	A hard effort
Total distance	10 miles

Vale of Glamorgan Fartlek

Steve Jones

Ex-world-record holder marathon, half-marathon
PRs: 13:18 (5K); 27:39 (10K)

One of Jonesy's favorite workouts was a fartlek session near the Vale of Glamorgan, not far from where he grew up in Wales. Before setting the world record in the marathon while working full-time as a Royal Air Force mechanic, he often ran either a 7-mile or a 12-mile course. Jones typically ran about a dozen hard efforts, ranging from about 20 seconds to 2-1/2 minutes.

Jones did not time his hard running, because "it was all about effort. I ran from one tree to another. I liked it because there was no mental pressure" of having to go to the track and hit specific times. These fartlek workouts are different from running repeats or intervals.

"Fartlek really is what it means—speedplay. With fartlek, because the stress is off, I run how I feel. Sometimes I feel great, and run eyeballs out; sometimes I am sore, so it is almost like a semi-tempo run. I did not know how long the efforts were in terms of time; but I did them every week from the same tree to the same tree, the same house to the same house. I did it all the time. It was some sprints, and I would barely recover before the next one."

Steve Jones

Jones always knew what day of the week he was going to run his fartlek. It was always penciled into his training. "I did not wake up and say, 'Oh, I think I will do a fartlek today.' I knew I was going to do 4 × 5 minutes on a Monday, maybe fartlek or a race on Wednesday—the league meets or the traditional race day in the Air Force was Wednesday—and hills Thursday."

When Jones was one of the best runners in the world during the 1980s, there was, he said, a period during which he never got tired.

He was always able to recover before his next workout, meaning he got stronger and stronger until he broke the world record. Fartlek, he said, was one of his key sessions during those years.

12 efforts, ranging from about 20 seconds to 2-1/2 minutes

Pace	Varies depending on how you are feeling; these are not timed
Recovery	Varies
When to do	All year long
Total distance	10 miles

Holmenkollen and Sognsvann Forest Fartlek

Dave Welch

Coach of Priscilla Welch
  Olympic marathoner from Great Britain (now a U.S. citizen)
  World-record holder (2:26:41) for women's masters marathon

Dave Welch learned the value of fartlek running from Oslo's *Norskskiforbund* (the Norwegian Ski Association). The skiers would do fartlek training during the summer months in the Holmenkollen and Sognsvann forests on the edge of Oslo. Dave, and later Priscilla, for shorter versions of the workout, would join the Norwegians when the couple was based in Norway for military service.

The Holmenkollen forest sessions were fartlek in its truest form. The runners and skiers would meet at the forest, at the edge of Oslo, and do a couple of miles' warm-up. Then they would stop and stretch. During her career, Priscilla always followed that same pattern, which she learned in those early days: warm up, stretch, run. That is because, says Dave, stretching an unwarmed-up muscle can lead to more injuries than it prevents. During this fartlek workout, the club members would sometimes stop and stretch.

This workout was entirely unstructured. The group would sprint or bound up a hill, jog down, then run hard for roughly 800 meters on a flat stretch, jog for a while, then run hard again. It was all by feel.

Most of the session was on grass or dirt. But when the runners and skiers came to a road, they would run hard on it for a stretch. They would sometimes walk for recovery, down a hill, although the Norwegians were known for running down dry, rocky river beds. The total workout was up to 4 hours.

"The emphasis of this kind of fartlek is on play. It is a combination of speed, jogging, walking, and fun. It can be anywhere from 30 minutes to 3 to 4 hours."

Priscilla Welch

"This is an absolutely superb workout—one of the best workouts a runner can do. You develop nearly every energy system as well as your muscular strength. It is all included in there."

Dave Welch

What was the total distance? "I haven't a clue," says Welch. "We never thought about miles or speed or anything." The key to this workout, said Dave, is that runners can put in a large volume of training along with good quality without getting too fatigued. "I felt better at the end of 4 hours than after a 2-hour run. You actually include in this fartlek several units of training: a unit of endurance training, a unit of strength training, and a unit of speed training."

Runners wanting to incorporate a fartlek workout into their training should try to find a nice area to run in, Welch says. Make the fartlek relaxing, and mix up the hard and easy running as you see fit.

4-hour fartlek session in a forest

Recovery	Walking or jogging
Pace	Varies
When to do	Year round
Total distance	"Not a clue"

The Army Short Fartlek

Jason Stewart

Two-time World Cross Country team member
Member of Army World Class Athlete Program
PRs: 13:32 (5,000 meters); 7:58 (3,000 meters)

Jason Stewart and his Army teammates have had good success doing a short fartlek session after first running a solid 10.4-mile run. Three times a week Stewart finishes the run by doing roughly 15 seconds hard, followed by a short float, then another hard 15 seconds. This is usually done on dirt.

According to Stewart, it will take at least a month to get used to doing an up-tempo run followed by fartlek. "But I know it is what the doctor ordered in terms of strength over 10 kilometers."

For regular runners training for a road race, Stewart recommends doing 6 to 10 miles at an increased pace, "one where it is slightly faster than where you'd be comfortable talking with running partners. Our runs have become silent affairs. All you hear is feet hitting the pavement." Then do the fartlek of roughly 10 to 12 hard efforts.

Someone running 90 miles would do 10 miles at the increased tempo before the fartlek. A runner averaging around 70 miles a week would do 8 miles, then the fartlek. Those averaging 50 miles or less would do 6 to 7 miles preceding the fartlek.

This will help make you a better runner by building strength without destroying your body or your mind, Stewart said. He has run 13:44 for 5K indoors and made the World Cross Country team off 4 months' worth of distance runs, strides, and judicious use of this fartlek session.

6 to 10 miles, followed by a fartlek session of short sprints

Pace	Hard
Recovery	Roughly 15 seconds between each effort
When to do	Winter and spring
Total distance	10 to 15 miles

Meyer-Rodgers Fartlek

Bill Rodgers

Four-time winner Boston Marathon
Four-time winner New York City Marathon
Former U.S. marathon record holder
Former world record holder, 25K

Bill Rodgers was never much of a fartlek runner, doing the bulk of his speed training on the track. However, in 1982 he and fellow Boston Marathon winner Greg Meyer several times incorporated a fartlek workout into their long runs. During a 20 to 21 mile run, the pair would run eight three-minute surges. The run ended with a hard final mile on the track, right at five-minute mile pace.

"Greg and I took turns leading during the three minute surges, and we took up to seven minutes between the surges to recover," explains Rodgers.

The training worked. That year, Rodgers won the Melbourne Marathon in 2:11:08, while Meyer ran 2:10:59 in winning the Chicago Marathon.

"I'm sure those workouts played a role. My last half (of the marathon) was faster than my first."

Bill Rodgers

One key to Rodgers' success was that he was one of the best downhill runners ever. When preparing for Boston, he would gear his training to the hills that come late in the race.

"My high school, coach, Frank O'Rourke, taught me to push hard after cresting a hill and to use the downhill. Before Boston I would occasionally add, say twice a week, repeats at a steady but not hard pace up and down hills on my courses."

Long run incorporating 8 x 3-minute surges

Recovery	Roughly 7 minutes between surges
Pace	Hard effort
Total distance	20 to 21 miles

Coogan's Marathon Strength Workout

Mark Coogan

Olympic marathoner, 1996
Silver medal, Pan American Games Marathon
Eight-time U.S. World Cross Country team member
USA Running Circuit winner, 1996
PRs: 13:23 (5K); 28:13 (10K)

One of Coogan's key workouts when preparing for a marathon is an 18-mile run with three long repeats during the run. After a 20-minute warmup and then some stretching, Coogan alternates 15 minutes of hard running at his marathon race pace with roughly 5 minutes of easy recovery. Coogan will cover between 3 miles and 5K during the hard effort.

"I try to do this on a rolling course. This is a strength workout that is all about time and effort. You don't have to get caught up in the exact time or distance you are running, but you do need to work hard. It is a long effort."

Mark Coogan

This workout can be done anywhere. When he lived in Boulder, Coogan ran the first hard effort slightly downhill down Monarch Road before turning north and ending somewhere around the IBM plant. The next segment would be all on dirt roads near the reservoir. The last hard effort would start at the bridge at N. 49th Street and end up back at the reservoir parking lot, where the workout started.

Coogan runs one long run and one medium-long run a week. This workout takes the place of the medium run. Coogan typically runs this session twice during his marathon buildup, once early on and again as the marathon nears.

"Hopefully I will feel a bit of progress in the way I feel. I've run this alone, but I'd rather go with people. I like this workout because you have to concentrate; 15 minutes is a long time to be running hard, and if you can do it in the workout, it will help you in the marathon. If you run this well, it gives you confidence in your training and racing."

Mark Coogan

In a variation of this workout before the 2000 Olympic trials marathon (in which he placed third), Coogan ran 12 miles at a solid 6-minute mile pace, then 3 × 3 miles in an accurate 4:55-per mile pace (the course was measured with a wheel). The total run was 25 miles. That workout will be too much for most people. Coogan recommends modifying it by doing three to five 8-minute surges at roughly marathon race pace during a medium-long run.

Three 15-minute efforts during an 18-mile long run

Pace	Marathon race pace
Recovery	5 minutes between each effort
Total distance	18 miles

The Wolfpack Fartlek

Rich Castro

Founder of the Boulder Road Runners

Coach of hundreds of runners, including Los Angeles marathon winner
  Rolando Vera

One of the key elements used by Castro since he started coaching—first on the college level (one of his early athletes was Mary Decker) and then with professional runners—has been group running. Quoting Rudyard Kipling, Castro says, "The strength of the wolf is in the pack, and the strength of the pack is in the wolf." That is what group running is all about; it can be a very powerful tool."

This group fartlek workout is designed to help runners get used to a change of tempo. Castro's runners meet at parking area of a large open space area. After warming up together, Castro designates different runners to lead each of the fast segments. First comes 5 × 45 seconds of hard running, followed by two sets of 1, 2, 3, 2, 1 minutes hard, with a minute recovery between each. The exact times are flexible; more important is getting all the hard efforts in.

"You will often see Kenyans doing this; that is where I got the idea," Castro says. "The Scandanavians also do a lot of this." Castro now uses this workout with some of the non-elites he coaches, because it allows them to get in a hard workout in a short time.

Runners who have a difficult time starting out at a hard pace are appointed by Castro to lead the shorter segments. Others who are leery of running at the front of the pack might be asked to lead the longest segments, to get them used to leading. "This workout is a good way to expose runners to these things," Castro says. "That is the role of the coach, to expose different aspects of racing. Performance is a different idea than fitness."

"I focus on time and effort during this session, trying to gear the hard segments to the effort a runner puts in during a 5K race. That is why the program works across the board; it doesn't matter if you are running 15 minutes for 5K or 20 minutes. The goal is to keep the workout limited to no more than 20 minutes of hard intensity."

Rich Castro

5 x 45 seconds of hard running, followed by two sets of 1, 2, 3, 2, 1 minutes hard

Recovery	One minute recovery between each effort
Pace	Roughly 5K race pace
Total distance	9 to 10 miles

Kardong's Road Fartlek

Don Kardong

4th place, 1976 Olympic Marathon
PR: 2:11:16 (marathon); 12:57.6 (3-mile); 4:01.9 (mile)
Road Runners Club of America "Road Runner of the Year" (1976)
3rd place, 1970 NCAA cross country championships
Winner of numerous road races, including Peachtree 10K, Honolulu Marathon and Le Grizz 50 Mile Ultramarathon.

This was one of Kardong's favorite and hardest workouts, although not his hardest. That would have been 20 quarters with one-minute rest, with a best average of 61.5 seconds. "That was in college, when I was tough."

Kardong did not do much pure fartlek, saying it was "a little too unstructured for me unless I had a group to run with, a scenario that pretty much disappeared after graduation from college." He did run some 20 to 30 minute fartlek workouts on a golf course but explains, "I got tired of dealing with golfers, who for some reason thought they belonged there."

One of Kardong's successful workouts was "somewhere between a track workout and a fartlek workout." After a 15-minute warmup, Kardong would run sets of 2 minutes-1 minute-30 seconds on one of his standard road courses. He took 90 seconds recovery after the 2-minute effort, one minute after the 1-minute effort, and 30 seconds after the 30-second effort. He would then immediately jump into the next set.

"I liked using time because it's easy to keep track of on a digital watch. This had some of the advantages of fartlek, since I was relieved of the mental burden of trying to run a certain precise distance in a certain time, and I wasn't confined to an oval. And it had the advantage of a track workout in that there was structure to it, which I found helpful. I also liked the mix-up of distances."

Don Kardong

The exact distance was not measured, but when he was an international competitior, Kardong would run roughly a half mile, quarter mile, and 200 meters for the segments. "These were hard, faster-than-race-pace, with enough recovery that my breathing was mostly back to normal after each interval," he explains. "On a good day I'd do five sets, at which point I was worn out and 10 miles was about completed. I may have done six sets now and then."

Another plus of the workout is that it is easily adaptable, Kardong adds. "You can adjust the effort, time between intervals, time between sets, number of sets, etc." He would sometimes start the sets with the 30-second effort, and at other times run 5 × 5 minutes.

"A good start for a recreational runner might be 2 to 3 sets, with plenty of rest between. The one caveat is to make sure you have a flat course. Sprinting downhills in particular is very risky."

Five sets of 2 minutes-1 minute-30 seconds

Recovery	90 seconds recovery after the 2-minute effort; 1 minute after the 1-minute effort; 30 seconds after the 30-second effort
Pace	Faster than race pace
Total distance	10 miles

4

Chapter 4

Interval Workouts: The Need for Speed

If you are a runner and are training to race well, you will, sooner or later, do intervals. There is really no way to get around it. These are a series of fast efforts on the track, with a minimum of recovery between each effort. You get in oxygen debt on the fast effort and repay only a part of that debt during the recovery. That means you are running hard again before being fully recovered.

Why do intervals? They are great anaerobic training, allowing you to increase your ability to hold a faster pace for a longer period of time. Intervals are the quickest way to get fit, but they carry with them an increased risk of injury because of the stress the fast running puts on your muscles, joints, tendons, and ligaments. Intervals should not be done until your body is strong enough to handle them.

"The number-one thing in running is consistency," Frank Shorter explains. "And it all centers on interval training. I can't tell you how many (intervals) to do. You have to find your own level. It comes down to this: Once or twice a week you run your butt off."

What a great way to describe intervals—"running your butt off." Shorter provides some simple advice, yet it is sometimes difficult to implement. How many intervals to do? What distance? How much recovery? Those are questions runners have asked since German coach Woldmar Gerschler first made extensive use of interval training in the 1940s in coaching Rudolph Harbig to the 800-meter world record.

When he was at his peak, Shorter ran intervals three times a week as part of his weekly 140 miles. He says one interval session a week is enough for those of you putting in 40 to 50 miles weekly. As you get in better shape you will want to run more mileage, "because you need it to support the more difficult and intense intervals."

Shorter became a champion in part because he could push himself to his limit on his hard days. Sometimes he ran intervals by himself; other times he did them with fellow Olympians Steve Prefontaine, Jack Bacheler, or Jeff Galloway.

Running intervals is usually easier with a group. There are many running groups that meet at tracks around the country before warming up and doing their interval workout together.

Once you decide you are going to do an interval session, the question becomes, how many and what length intervals to do? There are many different answers to this. Shorter recommends gearing all of your intervals to your race pace for 5,000 meters. The reason is to keep your leg rate as fast or faster than race pace.

For example, if your time for a 5K race is 19 minutes, your intervals—no matter what the length—should not be slower than 6-minute-mile pace, or 90 seconds for each 400 meters.

By Shorter's reckoning, someone who runs a 5K in 15:30 would thus do his or her intervals at 75 seconds per 400 meters. By coincidence, that is just about the pace that Ingrid Kristiansen ran her intervals when she set the 5K and 10K world records. "I am not a big believer in doing a large volume of intervals," Shorter said. "This enables you to do the workout and be very, very consistent."

Some coaches have their athletes—even high schoolers—do monster interval workouts. We runners, being a motivated bunch, can do those for a while. With that approach, however, Shorter says you might "start waking up and your first thought is, How can I get out of the workout today? So you need to have a program where that is not going to happen."

When it comes to determining the exact workout, Shorter says there might be some physiological benefit to doing 16 or 20 quarter-miles instead of 8 or 10. However, the psychological part is that you might not keep the training going year in and year out if the workload becomes too much, physically or mentally. De Castella agrees, saying that "staying on top of your running" is critical to long-term success.

Whatever the specific workout—whether short and fast 200- or 400-meter intervals, or longer 800-meter or mile repeats, "always make the interval attainable," urges Shorter.

You must find an interval workout that suits your personality. If you prefer running a ladder, such as a mile, half, quarter, and 200, do the longest repeat at the beginning of the workout. "I do that because I like the feeling of running faster as I go along," Shorter says. "Going harder and faster. Like a race. It is learning how to dole out your effort.

"Runners are creatures of habit. Runners are also creatures of even intensity. You get a sense of speed and effort from the intervals. Running hard at the end is fun.

"My goal was to get done with the last interval, have it be the fastest one in the workout, and be so exhausted that if someone came up and put a gun to my head and said 'Do another one,' I'd say, 'Shoot me.' You can't always do it, but that's the goal."

And what happens if you are feeling a bit fatigued when the time comes for the intervals? "Half the distance and maintain the speed. That way you can complete the workout."

Why not just skip the interval session and do it another day? For this simple reason: When race day comes along you might be feeling poorly once again, and you will not be able to postpone the race. "That is what happened to me in Montreal (at the 1976 Olympic Games)," Shorter said. "You have to learn to work through your lousy days."

"Running your butt off," "staying on top of your running," and "working through your lousy days"—sound advice for those who want to make interval training part of their regular workout schedules.

Masback's Mitochondrial Change of Pace

Craig Masback
3:52.7 miler
CEO of USA Track and Field

Masback, like many long-distance runners, is intelligent. One day, he and his college roommate, a medical student at Princeton, were sitting in their dorm room talking about training, analyzing why they were doing certain workouts.

The pair had an interval session of 400-meter repeats planned. "Craig, why do we run quarters?" the roommate asked.

Not satisfied with the answer "everybody else does them," Masback and his roommate put their heads together and decided 300-meter intervals would better suit their needs. "We wanted to stress the system more specifically," Masback explains. "There are different energy systems needed in middle-distance running. You stress specific systems in specific workouts, and we wanted to do what we would actually be doing in a race."

The workout they devised started with 6 × 300 meters with a 2-minute rest. Then there would be 4 × 1,100 meters, broken up by running 800 meters aerobically, then running the last 300 as hard as they could.

At the beginning of the season, the 800s were run in 2:15, capped by a 45-second 300-meters. When Masback was in midseason form, the 800s were run in 2 minutes and the 300 in 40 seconds.

"This was a specific workout for a change in rhythm, change of pace. We'd be running the 800s at a relaxed pace, then go all out. It was doing something on the mitochondrial level."

Craig Masback

Aerobic/anaerobic 1,100 meter intervals

Recovery	2-minute rest between each repeat
Pace	Faster than your mile-race pace on the 6 × 300s. On the 4 × 1,100 meters, the first 800 meters are run aerobically and the last 300 as hard as you can go
Total distance	10 miles, with warm-up and cool-down

10 X 10K

Arturo Barrios

Five-time world-record holder
Current world-record holder in hour run on the track
Two Pan American Games gold medals
Two fifth-place finishes in Olympic 10,000 meters
Coach of the U.S. Army's World Class Athlete Program
PRs: 27:08.6 (10,000 meters); 2:08:37 (marathon)

The favorite workout for Barrios was $10 \times 1,000$ meters on the track, with a slow lap jog recovery.

The reason Barrios liked this workout was that if he was able to average somewhere in the low 2:40s for the kilometers, with the last two always a bit faster, he knew he was in great shape to race.

> "This workout was the key. It really gave me a lot of confidence; after running 10 1Ks back to back, I knew all I had to do was put them together on race day."
>
> Arturo Barrios

Barrios ran this workout every other week starting in the spring and stopping 2 weeks before he left to race in Europe. Each week, he would get faster on the kilometers, a good indication that he was getting stronger. Then, when Barrios averaged in the low 2:40s for each K, he says, "I knew I was ready to break 28 minutes any time."

Many runners, even elite ones, have a tendency to run too fast on these long intervals, says Barrios. He gives the example of seeing 31- or 32-minute 10K runners at the track doing their 1K repeats faster than he did when he set his world record.

Regular runners can use the same principles in the training as the elites, Barrios says, although the amount and intensity of their intervals will be less. One reason for doing intervals, he adds, is to learn a change of pace. "Some people could not change their pace even if there was an earthquake or a monster chasing them."

Another way to learn to change your pace is striding 10×100 meters after your easy runs, Barrios says. The interval workout and the strides will help you finish faster and ensure that you can change the pace in the middle of your race.

According to Barrios, runners of all levels should keep in mind that consistency is the key in getting ready for any race. He rarely missed a day, and says keeping a training log is a good way to keep yourself on schedule. "You have to be religious with your training, going out even when it snows, rains, or is cold. This will be reflected when you race."

For more coaching tips from Barrios, see www.teambarrios.com.

10 x 1 kilometers

Recovery	A slow lap jog
Pace	A few seconds per mile faster than 5K-race pace (cut the workout down to 5-8Ks depending on your strength)
Total distance	10 miles, with warm-up and cool-down

Guerra's Confidence Builder

Silvio Guerra

Boston Marathon 2nd-place finisher
Four-time gold medalist, South American Games
Two-time Olympian (1996, 2000)
Ecuadorian national record holder, every distance from 3000 through marathon
PRs: 2:09:48 (marathon); 27:46 (10,000 meters)

Guerra's most important track workout is 8×1 kilometer with 2 minutes to 2:30 recovery. The times vary depending on Guerra's workload and the time of season.

Guerra favors this workout because, he says, it provides a runner with speed and endurance. In addition, it is "not too long and not too short." Guerra starts this workout with a 3-mile warm-up that ends at a quick pace. Then he always stretches for a solid 15 minutes before doing 10 strides.

Guerra runs this workout the Tuesday before a Sunday race. In addition to the physical benefits accruing from the session, Guerra gets confidence when he is able to run it very fast. As with Arturo Barrios, it is his way of verifying that he is in great shape.

"Mentally, I always get ready for this workout. It is tough, but it is very important."

Guerra's advice to runners wanting to do this workout is not to worry so much about the exact time. What is important is to push when it is the day to push hard; run easy when it is time to run easy.

> "That is the secret—recovering in time for your next workout. For me the focus is on recovering from the last workout and being ready for the next one. You need to be constant in your training."
>
> Silvio Guerra

It does not matter how fast you will be running your next 10K race, whether it is 28 minutes or 58 minutes—this principle is still the same.

The workout: 8 x 1 kilometer

Recovery	2 minutes to 2:30
Pace	Varies, but always hard
Total distance	10 miles

Pre's 30-40 Workout: Advanced Interval Training

Bill Dellinger

1964 Olympic bronze medalist (5,000 meters)

Ex-coach, University of Oregon

Coach of 14 conference and five NCAA cross country team champions

Coach of Steve Prefontaine

Oregon state high school cross country champion 1967-68

State mile champion, 1969, two-mile champion, 1968-69

Three-time NCAA cross country champion

Four-time NCAA 5,000-meter winner

Former American record holder, 2,000 through 10,000 meters

This workout, popularized by the late Prefontaine, consists of 3 miles of alternating 200 meters, run in 30 seconds, with 200 meters in 40 seconds. It is just one of the workouts in what Bill Dellinger calls *advanced interval training*. What is crucial in these sessions is the amount of rest the runners take.

Dellinger is one of the outstanding figures in American track and field. His career as a competitive runner started when the general principles guiding long-distance running were being formulated. He passed those principles along to his athletes during his years at the University of Oregon, where he coached Prefontaine and Alberto Salazar, among others.

The genesis for the 30-40 workout came at the 1956 Melbourne Olympic Games.

One day, Dellinger watched Vladimir Kuts of the Soviet Union doing a workout around a cricket field. Kuts would sprint a straightaway down the field, then jog around a curve, then sprint part of the next straight, then jog again. "He was doing a bunch of stuff that I saw him use in the 10,000 meters," says Dellinger.

Kuts went on to use an uneven pace to destroy Gordon Pirie of Great Britain in winning the 1956 10,000-meter gold medal.

In the 40-30 workout, Dellinger's runners start off with a 40-second 200 meters, immediately followed by a 30-second 200 meters. "All the guys start out at 40-30, and do that until they can no longer handle it," explains Dellinger. Once they fall off from 40-30, their workout ends. Some runners would go five or six laps. Others, quite a bit more. The most ever done? Prefontaine, who made 18 laps of 40-30. Salazar's best was 16 laps, and Steve Savage did 14 laps. Dellinger's team would do this workout two or three times during the winter.

> "This is just part of the training. We had a lot of drills. None of them was more important than the others. Another one we did was the 800-300 drill."
>
> Bill Dellinger

That drill consists of 800 meters at a runner's goal pace 5K, then a 400-meter recovery; then 300 meters at mile-race pace, then a 200 recovery in 40 seconds; then another 800 as the cycle repeats.

These kinds of sessions are also called *race simulation* workouts, because they mimic race conditions. The idea, Dellinger says, is to teach runners to recover while they are running.

Another simulation workout was done by Alberto Salazar, consisting of alternating 4:30/5-minute miles on the Adidas Oregon trail. Salazar started with a 5-minute mile before going right into a 4:30 mile. "Alberto did 7 miles of that," Dellinger says. "Recovery was what we were concerned with."

Adds Dellinger, "I think it is a lot tougher to do 5×400 meters in 60 seconds with a short rest than 8×400 meters in 60 with a 2-minute recovery." Dellinger says he did not use Pre's workout to judge what time Prefontaine might run in an upcoming race. Rather, "we did it to get used to uneven running. It was just part of the training, 14 minutes of uneven running."

Why is the rest critical in these workouts? Because "when you are in a race, you will not be able to stop. You have to learn how to recover while running, and you have to keep moving during the recovery session."

Dellinger says that runners wanting to do a race simulation workout can start out with 400-meter repeats at their goal pace for 5K. Start with a 200-meter recovery in 1 minute. Then bring the recovery down to 50 seconds. Dellinger advises that "as you get in better shape, you will cut the recovery down," rather than trying to run the intervals faster and faster.

Another simulation drill was described by Dellinger in a 1984 *Runner's World* article. The drill was done by Jim Hill, then one of the top U.S. 5,000-meter runners. In 3 miles of continuous running, Hill started with three laps in 3:09, followed by a half-mile recovery in

(continued)

Pre's 30-40 Workout:
Advanced Interval Training (continued)

2:40. Then came a 2:04 two-lapper, with an 80-second 440 for recovery. Next was a 440 in 60 seconds, with an 80-second 440 for recovery, followed by two laps of 40-30.

Hill's time for the 3 miles was 13:42. "That is excellent in itself," Dellinger wrote, "but the real significance of the drill is that Jim was below world-record pace for a total of seven laps spread across the 12 he ran." Asked about that workout now, Dellinger says, "It is the same principle: to get used to uneven running."

3 miles of alternating 30-second and 40-second 200 meters

Recovery	200 meters in 40 seconds
Pace	5K-race goal pace
Total distance	9 miles

300-Meter Intervals

Libbie Hickman

Former U.S. 5,000-meter, 10,000-meter champion
1999 USA Running Circuit championship
2000 Olympics 10,000-meter runner
World Championship 10,000- and 5,000-meter finalist

Hickman is one of the most versatile American runners, competitive from the 5,000-meters through the marathon. One of her key workouts is 8 × 300 meters, run in 48 seconds with a 200-meter recovery.

Hickman starts with a 20-minute warm-up, and she always makes sure she stretches before doing some 80-meter strides and then starting the workout. Hickman tries to be fairly well recovered before each 300 meters.

This is a workout Hickman ran before winning the 1999 U.S. 5,000-meter track title. "This is one of Libbie's tougher workouts, and we don't do it all season long," her husband Walter explains. "That would be too much."

Runners need to have a base before trying a workout like this. Hickman is unique in that she uses cross country to build her base in the winter months. She typically runs a fall marathon. After taking a long break, she does several months of cross-country skiing, up to 3 hours a day. It is a nonpounding, aerobic workout, Hickman explains, that helps give her the strength to do intervals later on in the year.

8 x 300 meters

Recovery	200-meter jog
Pace	800-meter race pace
Total distance	10 miles

The Alberto Salazar Special

Marc Davis

Ex-U.S. record holder for 2 miles (8:12)

U.S. road 5K record holder (13:28)

Two-time NCAA champion

1992 high school cross country National champion

1993 U.S. National Steeplechase champion

1996 Olympic steeplechase finalist

1998 U.S. National 5,000 meter champion

One of Davis' toughest workouts consists of a hard mile, then 1200, 800, and 400 meters. The recovery is half the distance of each segment; the mile is followed by a two-lap recovery, the 1200 by a lap-and-a-half recovery, and the 800 by a lap recovery.

Davis tries to run the workout as close to 4-minute-mile pace as possible. The best he ran was in 1995, on the track at Hayward Field in Eugene, Oregon. Davis clocked 4:06 for the mile, followed by a 3:01 for 1200 meters and 1:56 for 800 meters before finishing up with a 54-second 400 meters. He was so happy when he finished that he threw his spikes in the air and jogged around the track yelling and hitting the fence with his spikes. Soon afterward, Davis went to Europe and set his American record for 2 miles, as well as personal bests of 7:38 (3000 meters) and 3:36 (1500 meters).

Other athletes do this workout as well. The best time I've heard was done by Kenyan 2-mile world-record holder Daniel Komen, who ran splits of 3:59, 2:55, 1:53, and 53 seconds.

This is a good workout for people racing a mile through 5K, Davis says; it would not be as key a workout for 10K runners. It is beneficial because it combines strength and speed.

"This is an Alberto Salazer special I do a week out before going to Europe. The progression of the workout follows how a race often develops; you go out in 60-second pace and are anaerobic, then you have to go on faster and faster until on the last quarter you are just kicking. It is just a great workout that can tell you where you are. You are real tired and still have to kick. When I run this well, I know I can run pretty fast and strong."

Marc Davis

A fast ladder

Recovery	Half the distance of each segment (1 × mile, 1 × 1,200 meters, 1 × 800 meters, 1 × 400 meters)
Pace	As close to mile-race pace as possible
Total distance	9 miles
When to do	When peaking

Wetmore's Secret Intervals (or 5K Goal Pace 500s)

Adam Goucher

NCAA cross country, indoor 3,000-meter and outdoor 5,000-meter champion
U.S. national 5,000-meter, indoor 3,000-meter, and 4K and
  12K cross country champion
Third-fastest American over 5,000 meters (13:11)
2000 Olympic trials 5,000-meter champion

This workout consists of 10 × 500 meters on the track, with a 100-meter jog across the track between each repeat. Goucher and his training partner, Alan Culpepper, run a 3-mile warm-up, then do some stretching and eight strides.

Each 500 meters finishes around the first turn from the start; after each repeat the pair jogs straight across the grass infield back to the starting line. As soon as they get there, it is time to start again. Goucher runs the 500s in 1 minute, 16 seconds to 1:18, going through the first 400 meters in 61.5 to 62 seconds. His best time for the 5,000 meters of fast running (the 10 × 500 meters) is 12:58, run 4 weeks before he won the 1999 U.S. national 5K title.

Goucher calls this workout "Coach Wetmore's secret. It gives you good preparation for racing 5K. You can crank it down faster and faster, decreasing the rest. I like it because you can figure out where you are in your training."

The first time Goucher runs this workout is after his 3 months of winter base training. In that first workout, he and Culpepper take 1-minute recovery between each of the 500-meter repeats.

"Every time we run it we decrease the rest. When Al and I get to the point where we are taking 35 to 38 seconds of rest, we know we are near our peak performance and our peak fitness. This workout makes me feel good and fast and hard."

Adam Goucher

Goucher advises regular runners wanting do to this workout to "slow it down and adjust it to their level." He also says you must fit it into the proper phase of your training. "It is a great workout. When I ran 12:58 I knew I was pretty fit."

Runners doing this workout should aim for their sea-level goal pace, Wetmore says. "This is a good, deep anaerobic workout." You should start with the amount of recovery that allows you to complete the workout, then reduce the recovery as the weeks go by.

10 x 500 meters

Recovery	100-meter jog in 1 minute; decrease amount of rest each time workout is run
Pace	Sea-level goal pace for 5K
Total distance	9 miles

Kenahs' Key Workout

Rich Kenah

World Championships indoor 800-meter bronze medal
World Championships outdoor 800-meter bronze medal
Member four World Championship teams
NCAA indoor champion
Seven-time NCAA All-American
Junior national 800-meter champion
Junior Pan American 800-meter champion
2000 Olympic 800-meter runner
PRs: 1:43.38 (800 meters); 3:37.17 (1,500 meters)

Cheri Kenah

11-time NCAA All-American
3-time NCAA runner-up
Member of two World Championship teams
Ranked No. 1 in U.S. (5,000 meters, 1999)
PRS: 15:10 (5,000 meters); 4:30.10 (mile); 4:09.23 (1,500 meters)

Rich Kenah's workout is 4 × 400 meters with 4 minutes' rest.

According to Kenah, "There is no magic workout. An entire plan is necessary to race well consistently." With that in mind, this is a workout Kenah does as he nears his racing season. When Kenah runs all four 400 meters in 52.0 seconds, he knows he is ready to race a top-level 800 meters or mile.

In a similar way, Kenah's wife, Cheri, knows she is ready for a good 3000 or 5000 meters when she can run the 3 × 1 mile in 4:45.

These workouts simulate the "pain you will get in the last third of our races," Rich Kenah says. "They are a simple but effective workout, and a great barometer of our fitness."

The workouts start with about a 1-hour warm-up routine that includes jogging, strides, drills, and stretches. This session comes after a month of "fairly high volume" in Florida (between 60 to 90 miles a week for Rich and 70 to 100 for Cheri). "There is no magic number for weekly mileage," he says.

Kenah says that regular runners can "absolutely" use this workout. He advises running the intervals at a controlled effort and shooting for your goal pace for 100 to 150 percent of your race distance. For example, someone wanting to run 800 meters in 2 minutes 30 seconds would run the 400s in 75 seconds. A runner aiming for 2 minutes for 800 meters would attempt to hit the 400s in 60 seconds.

To emulate Cheri's workout, runners aiming for a 15:30 5K would try to hit each of their miles in roughly 5 minutes.

4 x 400 meters or 3 x 1 mile

Recovery	4 minutes of jogging between each 400 m or mile repeat; no walking
Pace	Race goal pace
Total distance	7 or 9 miles

Rainey's 300s

Merideth Rainey Valmon

800 meter best of 1:57.04

Two-time NCAA 800-meter champion

1992, 1996, Olympic 800-meter runner

Three-time U.S. National outdoor 800-meter champion

Four-time U.S. National indoor 800-meter champion

Pan American Games gold medalist

Rainey Valmon's key workout is 3 × 300 meters, in varying speeds and with varying recoveries.

This is a workout that can be modified and done all year long. "It is extremely versatile because for any distance race the last 300 meters is critical if it is a tight race," Merideth explains.

During her base-training phase, Rainey Valmon recommends running 3 to 4 sets of 3 × 300 meters at a slower pace, but jogging only 100 meters in between. "The first (300) is comfortable, the second one takes some effort, and the third teaches you to lift and accelerate even when fatigued," Rainey Valmon says.

During the spring, the number of sets decreases, as do the times on each 300. When you are in good shape, Rainey Valmon says, aim to run all three 300s within each set a little bit faster than your target time for the last 300 of your race—but always keeping the recovery to the same 100-meter jog/walk.

When you are nearing race day and running the 300s very fast, take a full recovery between sets. Rainey Valmon explains that the between-set recovery is not important; rather, it is the time on each 300 and the amount of recovery between each repeat that is key.

"The most important thing is learning to be tough on that third one. You will feel similar to how you feel at the end of a race, which is TIRED. This workout trains the athlete to run a target time for a strong finish to a race even in debt."

Merideth Rainey Valmon

Sets of 3 x 300 meters

Recovery	Varies depending on the season; during base phase, 100-meter jog
During season	100-meter walk
When peaking	A full recovery
Pace	Varies depending on the season; during base, comfortable; during season, target pace for last 300 meters of race
When peaking	Fast
Total distance	7 to 8 miles

Hogen's Pyramid

Dieter Hogen

Coach of three-time Boston Marathon winner Uta Pippig and Sammy Lelei (2:07:02 marathoner)

For runners wanting to increase their speed for a mile, 3K, or 5K, Hogen recommends a workout consisting of a fast 800 meters, followed by a 4-minute jog; a fast 600 meters with a 3-minute jog; a fast 400 with a 2-minute jog, finishing up with a fast 200 meters. All at faster than mile-race pace.

East German middle-distance runners used to get their speedwork in with this kind of pyramid training. The basic principle is that to run fast in a race, you must have run faster than your race pace during training. For most people, one speed session a week is enough, Hogen says, because too much very fast speedwork can lead to injuries. That is what happened to Hogen as a young runner, when he was forced by the East German bureaucracy to run too many races and do too much speedwork, leading to injuries that ended his career. He turned to coaching and fled East Germany with Pippig in 1990.

For those of you new to speedwork, Hogen recommends starting out with some 200- or 400-meter repeats. This will help your running form and get you used to faster training.

"Go out easy during the first part of the workout and push the last 200 meters. Do what your body can handle."

Dieter Hogen

800 meters, 600 meters, 400 meters, 200 meters

Recovery	4-minute jog; 3-minute jog; 2-minute jog
Pace	Faster than mile race pace
Total distance	7 miles

World Record Kilometers

Khalid Khannouchi

World-record holder marathon, 2:05:42

Two-time Chicago Marathon winner

1999 Road Runner of the Year

PRs: 1:00:27 (half-marathon); 27:45 (10K); 13:24 (5K)

Khalid Khannouchi puts the finishing touches on his pre-marathon preparations by running a workout of $12 \times 1,000$ meters in 2:40-2:42, with a 200-meter recovery. "That is his toughest workout. When Khalid can do that, we know he is fit. He knows he can win any race when he is this kind of shape," says his wife and coach, Sandra.

In the final months before a marathon, Khannouchi will also run $6 \times 2,000$ meters in 5:30 to 5:35. That is what Sandra call his "long training." For speed, his favorite workout is 25×400 meters, run in 61 seconds with a short recovery.

Sandra Khannouci explains that these sessions are part of Khalid's weekly mix of training. He builds up to the workout by running 125 miles a week, anchored by a long run of 18-22 miles. Every morning he runs 10 miles in 55-58 minutes, often on hilly trails near their home in New York; workouts are then done in the afternoon.

12 x 1,000 meters

Recovery	200-meter jog
Pace	2:40 to 2:42 per kilometer
Distance	13 miles

400s With a Fast Float

Rob de Castella

World record, marathon, 2:08:18
World Championship gold medal, 1983
Commonwealth Games gold medal, 1982, 1986
Track & Field News' Marathoner of the 1980s

Deek ran only a few different track sessions, most often 8×400 meters with 200 meters' fast float—not a jog—for the recovery. The 400s are at 5K-race pace or faster.

This was one of Deek's classic workouts, which he ran nearly every Tuesday morning for 15 years. This is a tough session because of the float. On each 400, you go over your anaerobic threshold—which Deek defines as your fastest maintainable speed—then dip just below your threshold on the recovery.

The workout starts with a 200 float and ends with a 400. That adds up to 5K of running, with the whole distance timed. Deek would run 15:30 for the 5K on a "bad day." An average workout was 14:30 to 15 minutes, and when he was in good form, he would run the session in 14 minutes. The times on the 400s would range from 63 seconds when de Castella was in peak shape for a championship race, to 69 or 70 seconds during the winter. The float was typically 45 seconds.

The popular de Castella was the center of a big training group wherever he went. Many runners would come and try to do this workout with him. They would be with Deek on the first few 400s; then the short rest would get to them and they would drop back. Eight by 400 meters might not look that tough on paper; try it with the quick float and then see what you think!

Deek says regular runners doing this session should slow the float down if necessary to keep the 400s at their goal pace.

World Championships marathoner Don Janicki did a similar workout. His was 12 x 400s with a fast 100-meter jog recovery. As with Deek's 400s, this is a quick and to-the-point session. Janicki would run it every Saturday before his Sunday long run. He usually averaged 67 to 68 seconds per 400. His best was 65 seconds per 400.

The workout: 8 x 400 meters

Recovery	200-meter float
Pace	5K race pace
Total distance	9 miles
When to do	All year long (with different emphasis, depending on the season)

Holman's 600s

Steve Holman

NCAA and U.S. national 1500-meter champion
1992 Olympic runner
PR: 3:31.52 (1500 meters; third fastest on U.S. all-time list)

Holman has different key workouts for different times of the year. This one is 4 × 600 meters with a 2:30- to 3-minute jog recovery, which he does in his final stages of preparing for a major race, just before starting to rest as part of his peaking process.

When Holman averages 1:22 to 1:23 for each 600 meters, he knows he is in "at least" 3:32 (for 1,500 meters) shape.

A variation of this workout is to run 3 × 600 with a 30-second jog, followed by a fast 200 meters. Holman takes a 3-minute recovery before each 600-200. Holman's goal is to hit the 600s in 1:22 or faster and the 200s in 26 seconds or faster.

Here is the key to these workouts. Not only do they physically help get Holman ready to race, they build his confidence by showing him how fit he is.

"For me, believing in my workouts is critical. When I run my favorite workout at a certain pace, I have a fairly accurate indicator of how fast I can race at that point. Having the knowledge of achieving specific benchmarks in practice definitely removes some of the anxiety about race performance for me."

Steve Holman

That is because after doing this workout, Holman tells himself heading into an important race, "I know I am capable of running very fast. I have already proved it in practice. Now, I simply have to execute."

Holman has worked with coach Frank Gagliano for many years, and he also worked closely with his agent, Kim McDonald, a former elite runner, and trained with many of the Kenyans McDonald represents. "I think the saying goes that learning is an ongoing process, just ask the dinosaurs—once you stop evolving, you become extinct."

Holman's training is geared to getting him to eventually run his goal of 3:28 for 1500 meters, which is 56 seconds per 400 meters. He says regular runners should build a strong base, or foundation, before attempting speedwork. Then you have to learn what works for you and what doesn't, and how hard you can train without breaking down. "I still like to experiment with new things, try exotic workouts occasionally, and modify things based on things other people have had success with. But basically I trust my coach to lead me to where I want to go, and every evening I want to be able to say to myself that I did everything I could that day to help me reach my goals."

4 x 600 meters

Recovery	2:30- to 3:00-minute jog
Pace	Faster than half-mile race pace
Total distance	8 miles, with warm-up and cool-down
When to do	When peaking

Repeat 800s

Frank Shorter

Olympic marathon gold and silver medals
U.S. national cross country champion (four times)
NCAA and U.S. national 6-mile champion

One of Frank Shorter's standard track workouts was 6 × 800 meters, starting at 2:09 and decreasing by 1 second each repeat. So the final 800 meters is run in 2:04. There is a lap jog in between each 800.

One reason Shorter liked running 800-meter intervals is because, he says, it is more difficult than running 12 by 400 meters. "That is a workout which will get you in shape, but the 800s are harder. You are really hanging out there on them."

The goal is to run each 800 progressively faster. Doing the workout that way not only shows you are in good shape; it also gives you a psychological boost. "You need a good day for them, and you have to be prepared."

Shorter recommends that people wanting to do this workout modify it and run 4 × 800 meters, at their 5,000-meter race pace. Make sure to run a second or two faster on each repeat. That is what Shorter did on all his intervals. For example, another workout he ran with Steve Prefontaine was a ladder consisting of a mile, three-quarters, a half and 4 × 400 meters. Because Shorter was racing 3 miles in the 12:50s (about 13:25 for 5K), he ran no slower than 63 seconds for his 400 meters (his 5K-race pace).

"That was the kind of workout we did," Shorter said. "Speed ruled."

Another half-mile interval session was 3:48-miler Ray Flynn's favorite workout. He would run 6 × 800 with a 3-minute recovery. When he could average 1:58 for the 800s, he knew he was ready for a good mile. "It is very demanding; it takes great endurance with not too long of a recovery to succeed at this workout."

Flynn did this workout in the early to middle part of his buildup for the track season. "It was not one to do in midseason but it was always a good barometer of where I stood," explains Flynn.

4-6 x 800 meters

Pace	Starting at your 5,000-meter race pace and decreasing by 1 second each repeat
Recovery	A lap jog in between each 800 meters
Total distance	8-9 miles, with warm-up and cool-down
When to do	After base-building phase of training

Brown's Championship Simulation Run

Jon Brown

British record holder 10,000 meters (27:18.14)
1996, 2000 Olympian
PRs: 13:19.78 (5000 meters); 2:09:44 (marathon); 1:01:47 (half-marathon)

This is Brown's key workout that he runs at least once a season—if he is fit enough. It consists of 3 by 2 kilometers/1 kilometer with 90 seconds' recovery between each repetition.

Brown started running this workout when he competed for coach Bill Bergan at Iowa State University; he has since modified it to make it a little harder. The reason Brown runs this workout is because it is a good indicator of both his 5K and 10K shape.

The session works like this: first, run a 2K at your 10,000 meter race pace, then increase your pace on the next repetition to your 5K pace. That way Brown gets in a 5-kilometer/10-kilometer-pace workout all in one, and it also trains his system to recover from a change of pace.

Brown says the hardest part of the workout is the 2 kilometers after the fast 1Ks, because with only 90 seconds in between the sets, you are still recovering during the next 2 kilometers.

Brown uses this workout during what he calls a "championship simulation exercise." He will first do a 12K tempo run to simulate a 10,000-meters semifinal, then 3 days later do this workout to simulate the 10,000 final. A good effort on this workout for Brown is running the 2Ks around 66 seconds per lap, and the 1Ks at 64 seconds per lap. When Brown ran his personal best of 27:18, he did the workout about 4 weeks before the race.

To make the workout manageable for regular runners, Brown suggests taking more recovery between the 2K/1K segments—however much you need so that the required 10K/5K pace can be maintained. For example, someone aiming for a 33-minute 10K would try to maintain 80-second lap pace on the 2Ks, followed by perhaps 77-second pace on the 1Ks.

"You don't need to do this workout too often!"

Jon Brown

3 sets of 2 kilometers/1 kilometers

Recovery	90 seconds' recovery between each set
Pace	10K goal race pace for the 2,000 meters, 5K goal pace for the 1,000 meters
Total distance	10 miles

Culpepper's Ladder

Shayne Culpepper

Two-time World Cross Country member
Three-time All-American track runner
Three-time NCAA All-American 2000 Olympic 1,500 meter runner
PRs: 2:03.3 (800 meters), 4:07.9 (1500 meters), 16:09 (5K)

When preparing for a mile or 1,500 meters on the track, Culpepper's key workout is two sets of 600 meters, 400 meters, 300 meters, 200 meters, 100 meters. There is about a minute-and-a-half jog between each repeat (very slow, about 100 meters), and 3 minutes between the two sets. The 600 meters is run at about mile pace, or a little faster. The 300, 200, and 100 meters are at roughly Shayne's 400-meter or 800-meter race pace.

Culpepper used to do this workout with a male training partner; now, she does it by herself or with All-American partners Carrie Messner and Kara Wheeler, or with U.S. Army runner Roxanne Bernstein. Culpepper likes doing this ladder workout because it is easier for her to get through than doing a set of repeats.

"If I had to try and do 800 (-meter) intervals . . . arrggh! That is because if I do something over and over I know how hard it will be. With the ladder I can trick myself a little bit."

Shayne Culpepper

Another ladder Culpepper runs when training for 5 kilometers is two sets of 1,000 meters, 800 meters, and 600 meters, all at race pace (about 75 seconds per lap). She ran this workout before the 2000 cross country nationals, where she placed fourth. "I do this ladder because one of my weak spots is 2- to 3-minute repeats. This really did help me get the pace, get in the groove of my 5K pace. The race was 4 kilometers, but in cross country that is more like a 5K on the track."

The ladders are done after Culpepper's base phase of training is finished. She did an abbreviated version of the workout a week before the 1999 U.S. national 1,500 meters, where she placed third. This was 500 meters, 400, 300, 200 meters, all at 60-second pace. She will continue to do both the long and the short ladders before racing a 5K on the track.

Runners of varying abilities can change this workout by focusing on whatever pace they plan on running in their race. For example, someone shooting for a 17-minute 5K might run the 600 meters in roughly 1:54 and the 400 meters in 75 seconds.

Two sets of 600 meters, 400 meters, 300 meters, 200 meters, 100 meters

Recovery	A very slow 100-meter jog between each repeat; 3-minute recovery between the sets
Pace	The 600 meters is run at mile pace, or a little faster The 300, 200, and 100 meters are a runner's 400-meter or 800-meter-race pace
When to do	During racing season
Total distance	6 miles

Bannister's Quarters

Sir Roger Bannister

First man under 4 minutes for the mile

1953 European champion, 1,500 meters

1954 Empire Games gold medalist, 1,500 meters

Bannister's key workout in his epic assault on the 4-minute-mile barrier was 10 × 400 meters in 59 seconds, with a 2-minute recovery. "I did this because it gives you stamina and speed," Bannister explains.

Bannister, a medical student studying at Oxford University, did not have much time to devote to his training. He tried to be as scientific as possible and came up with this intense interval workout as a way to get the most out of the 30 minutes he allowed himself for training each day.

Bannister worked his way up to the workout. In the spring of 1953, he was running 10 × 400 meters in 63 seconds, an effort that left him "exhausted for several days," Bannister wrote in *The 4-Minute Mile* (Lyons & Burford, 1989).

In the winter of 1954, with Australian John Landy already having come oh-so-close to the 4-minute mile, Bannister started running this workout faster. By the spring, he and training partners Chris Brasher and Chris Chataway had gotten their 400s down to 61 seconds. Then, just three weeks before the Oxford versus British AAA race, Bannister ran his 10 × 400 in 59 seconds, with the same 2-minute recovery. After freshening up and running a three-quarter-mile time trial, on May 6, Bannister clocked 3:59.4, breaking the 4-minute-mile barrier.

"I think most people go too fast in the beginning of the race. I think the thing they want to do is not to set off too fast at the start. After the half-mile, start moving up."

Roger Bannister

10 x 400 meters

Recovery	2 minutes
Pace	59 seconds
Total distance	3 miles

Tegen's "Emptying the Anaerobic Credit Card"

Suzy Favor Hamilton

Three-time Olympian
Three-time U.S. 1,500 meter champ
Three-time U.S. junior 1,500 meter champ
23-time Big 10 conference titles
Nine NCAA titles
14-time All American

One of Hamilton's key workouts is fast 800-meter intervals, a session she did several times during her stellar 2000 track season leading up to the Sydney Olympic Games.

The 800s are done once in a week or 10-day period of training when Hamilton "totally empties out the anaerobic capacity in order to create the stimulus to replenish it," explains her coach, Peter Tegen of the University of Wisconsin. Earlier in the season that anaerobic "emptying out" comes from 1,000 meter, 1,200 meter and mile intervals.

Hamilton often does her workouts on her own, with only Tegen for company. That way she is able to concentrate on her target pace. "I actually found training by myself is better," she said. "I like the one-on-one attention I get with my coach."

According to Tegen, the idea of this workout is "for that particular day within a cycle to take the anaerobic credit card limit all the way down to zero." The way the debt is paid off is often with the pain you go through while doing the hard workout, he said. This is a way to simulate the "incredible demands" Hamilton will go through in an international race. "So the idea of going through workouts like 800 meters is to get to the point where the body is already quite fatigued, and to top it off, do one more."

On her website, www.suzyfavorhamilton.com, Hamilton calls the 800 meter workout "very intense but very fun." In addition, she writes that her favorite workout for a 5K is a 20-minute hard tempo run once a week on the grass.

Finally, Hamilton offers the following insight, gained after the death of her brother, which is perhaps more important than any training tip:

> "Everytime I run, it is a gift. I want to live each day to the fullest."
>
> Suzy Favor Hamilton

800 meter repeats

Recovery	Full recovery
Pace	Close to all out
When to do	Later in preparation for track season

Chapter 5

Hill Workouts: Building Strength and Stamina

Triathlete Neill Woelk remembers riding hard up a very steep hill on Old Stage Road west of Boulder one hot summer morning. "Sweat was pouring down my eyes, I was pedaling away, and I was feeling terrible," Woelk recalls. "Then I hear this thump, thump, thump sound. I turned around and there was Deek [Rob de Castella], and he just flies past me going up that hill. He ran his hills very, very hard."

De Castella was not alone. Herb Elliot, Sebastian Coe, Steve Jones, Kip Keino, and Moses Tanui are good examples of athletes who have benefited from running hills, which build endurance and strength and can give you a solid anaerobic workout without the pounding of the track.

Hill workouts are not easy. Benji Durden, a coach and 2:09:59 marathoner who qualified for the 1980 Olympic team that boycotted the Moscow Olympics, recommends that those starting out on hills run five to seven hill repeats of 90 seconds, with a slow jog or walk down the hill in between each hard effort.

When doing your hill workout, "Your fitness level determines how hard you run them," said Durden. "You should never run them so hard that you can't keep the pace throughout the workout. That is a big mistake people make: they try to go all out and can't finish the workout."

And why do hill repeats help you? Simple, says Durden: "You get a very high cardiovascular workout with a fairly low skeletal-musculature stress." In other words, you get in deep oxygen debt without beating yourself up. By running hills, you will get stronger, stay healthy, and when you race will feel strong and powerful.

Hills are a workout that should be incorporated into your weekly training schedule. "You can do hills on a regular basis throughout the year," Durden advises. "Do them once a week for 3 to 6 weeks, several times a year. I would always have a period of time when I went back to the basics, and going back to the basics means running hill repeats."

Other coaches agree with Durden. Jon Sinclair says that hill training absolutely should be part of your regular training program "because it helps your body adapt to that ineffable stress you will feel when racing. If that is your goal—and it is not everyone's goal—but if it is, then there is a real benefit to doing hard hill workouts."

Masback's Ski Area Bounding

Craig Masback

3:52.7 miler
CEO USA Track & Field

Like many other successful runners, Craig Masback used the Lydiard concept of building a base in the preseason. Hills were a part of that. "My best workout was at a ski area in Vermont," he said.

The session was three sets of (1) bounding up a 600-meter hill; (2) running down to the bottom; and (3) sprinting up the hill.

"We repeated it, so it was bounding up the hill, running down, running up. At the end we'd do 12 by 100 meters. Then we'd go home and lie in bed."

Craig Masback

A circuit of bounding and then sprinting up a hill was also the way Dieter Hogen trained his East German athletes in their preseason. And Lasse Viren had a 1-kilometer circuit with a steep hill in a pine forest outside of his home in Myserkerla, Finland. He ran that each week in the early spring before stepping onto the track.

Three sets of alternating bounding up a 600-meter hill and sprinting up the hill

Recovery	Running down the hill
Pace	Hard
When to do	In preseason, before track season
Total distance	9 miles

Deek's Thursday Hill Session

Rob de Castella

World record, marathon, 2:08:18

World Championship marathon gold medal, 1983

Two-time Commonwealth Games marathon gold medal, 1982, 1986

Track & Field News' Marathoner of the 1980s

One of the foundations of de Castella's training program was the weekly hill session he ran every Thursday for roughly 15 years. He calls hill running "maybe the best overall training you can do. It makes you strong, helps you get faster, and improves your running form."

De Castella had a couple of different hill sessions. When training at the Australian Institute of Sport in Canberra, he would incorporate hills into a 10-mile fartlek run. His favorite loop had 12 hills of varying lengths. He would run the hills nearly all out.

While training in the United States, Deek's hill workout started with a 20-minute warm-up. Then came a 2-mile sustained run on the roads, in about 9:40. After a short 5- to 10-minute jog, he and his training partners would run 8 hill sprints: 4 × 40-second hill and 4 × 1-minute hill. The workout ended with a 20-minute cool-down.

Deek was not concerned about timing the hill sprints; effort is what mattered to him. He says that the greatest benefit from a hill workout comes when you sprint all out at the start of a short, fairly steep hill, rather than gradually picking up the pace and trying to sprint at the end. Running the hill Deek's way is more difficult, because lactic acid gets built up immediately, and a runner has to concentrate on holding his form the rest of the hill.

De Castella believes it is more valuable to run strongly and aggressively up a short hill than to go on a longer hill where you are more likely to lose your form and start jogging.

"Hills are a great way to simulate sprinting when you're tired at the end of a race."

Rob de Castella

2-mile tempo run followed by 8 short hill sprints

Recovery	Short jog between the 2-mile and the hills; jog down the hill after each sprint
Pace	Nearly all out
When to do	Year round
Total distance	10 miles

Sinclair's "Money Workout"

Jon Sinclair

Winner Peachtree 10K, Bloomsday 12K (twice), Columbus marathon, Virginia
 10-miler (four times)
Two-time U.S. Road Racer of the Year
Now coaching (contact: **www. anaerobic. net**)
PRs: 28:16 (10K); 13:35 (5K); 1:01:45 (half-marathon)

Sinclair's longevity as an elite runner is due in part to a hard run he did up the Rist Canyon west of Fort Collins in Colorado. The canyon is 8 miles long, divided into three sections, with a half-mile between each section. The total climb goes from 6,000 to 8,000 feet. The first section is 3 miles ending with a half-mile steep hill. This is followed by a half-mile jog. Then comes a 2-mile section, ending with a 600-meter "hellacious" hill. Then a mile jog. The final section is a mile and a half to the top; the last part is very steep.

"It is a long max-$\dot{V}O_2$ workout with hard anaerobic segments. It is very, very tough and simulates a lot of racing stress. As the workout goes along, the hard sections get shorter, you are getting zapped, and the altitude is getting higher, meaning there is more oxygen stress."

Jon Sinclair

How steep is it? Steep enough that at the end Sinclair is almost on his hands and knees. Sinclair calls this "a mean, real tough workout" and compares it to a difficult max-$\dot{V}O_2$ test "that gets tougher and tougher until you can't go anymore. It is so tough that your eyes are bulging out."

When he was one of the top U.S. road racers, Sinclair's pattern was to spend the winter training in New Zealand. When he returned, he would run Rist Canyon before the spring racing season. After racing most of the summer, he would resume doing this workout in the fall. The reason, he says, is that "it is a real good way to focus and give the racing stress that is needed to race. This helped as much mentally as anything. It increased your strength and you are running right at the $\dot{V}O_2$ level where you need to work at. I did this workout by myself mostly, because, honestly, not many people had the strength needed to get a workout out of it."

Running Rist Canyon was not Sinclair's favorite workout. "I dreaded it, but it produced good results. I called it my money workout. Cardiovascularly it is eye-bulging stress, the oh-my-god-I-can't-go-any-longer kind of stress. It is not done for speed, but for mental toughness. You have to be very focused to do this and you have to be ready for it."

'Hellacious' uphill run with three hard segments

Recovery	Half-mile recovery between each hard section (The first section is 3 miles, ending with a half-mile steep hill. This is followed by a half-mile jog. Then comes a 2-mile section, ending with a 600-meter "hellacious" hill. Then a mile jog. The final section is a mile and a half to the top; the last part being very steep.)
Pace	Hard enough to produce eye-bulging stress, the oh-my-god-I-can't-go-any-longer kind of stress
Total distance	8 miles
When to do	Before racing season begins

Wall Street 10-Miler

Melody Fairchild

Kinney prep national cross country champion
High school 3,000-meter record holder
1996 NCAA 3,000-meter indoor champion

Fairchild's favorite workout is an hour and 15 minutes of good, solid hills, often on a dirt road called Wall Street that goes through an old mining district in Colorado. On her hill runs, Fairchild says she learns how to pace herself, and she tries to run at her anaerobic threshold for as long as she can.

Fairchild is one of those runners who's good in cross country, track, and on the roads. The foundation of her success lies in hill running, which she says "is the greatest way to get in shape fast. You get instant feedback running up hills, and they are challenging."

There is no hiding on a hill.

"The second you start going up a hill you find out where you are at that day. They bring me to the point of maximum output if I run them hard. Hills are a challenge mentally, too."

Melody Fairchild

Fairchild's advice is to find a loop with several hills on it. When you get to a hill, don't run it all out. Rather, let the challenge of the hill come to you. Fairchild explains it like this: "The hill will take care of the workout and will get your heart rate up. It will make your hips and butt strong, which is where you get your explosiveness from."

And, she urges, do not run fast on the downhill. Save your hard running for the uphills.

One hour, 15-minute run over hills

Recovery	No recovery during the run
Pace	Solid on the hills, easy on the downhills
When to do	Year round
Total distance	10 miles

Carpenter's Perfect 20-Minute Workout

Matt Carpenter

USATF 2000 Mountain Runner of the Year
High-altitude marathon world-record holder, set at Everest Sky Marathon
Course record holder Pikes Peak Ascent, Pikes Peak Marathon

After a warm-up, run 20 minutes of 1 minute hard, 1 minute easy. Carpenter has done this workout twice a week for years: every Tuesday on the flats, every Thursday up a hill.

He calls it a "perfect workout," especially if you are traveling, because it can be done anywhere, anytime, on any kind of terrain. You do not need a track to get a good workout in, he says. "For a mountain runner, this is an invaluable workout because it can be done up hill and on trail. I strongly believe it helped get me where I am."

When Carpenter starts his racing season, there is a big spread from his easy minutes to his hard minutes. As he gets fitter and stronger, the easy minutes get faster, and the spread between the hard and easy minutes becomes less obvious.

"As this process occurs you are forced to learn your threshold limits, your recovery limits, and very precise pacing skills. These are the key elements to a successful race that every runner needs to learn no matter what level they are at."

Matt Carpenter

Although this workout is simple in concept, Carpenter says there is "almost no limit to what you can get from it with the slightest variations in how you do the easy minute." Variations on the workout include 30 or 40 minutes of 1 minute hard, 1 minute easy. Or, 2 minutes hard, 1 minute easy.

Carpenter advises people running this workout for the first time to set the timer on their watches to 1-minute repeats. Try to have all 10 hard minutes be consistent. People at first might run their easy minutes too hard in the beginning, meaning they will have to walk in order to recover later on. Carpenter says that is fine, as long as the quality of the hard minutes is kept up. "This is part of the learning process, with the goal being that all 10 easy minutes will also become consistent. Again, pacing is everything."

10 x 1 minute hard, over a variety of terrain

Recovery	1 minute between each hard effort
Pace	At your threshold
When to do	Throughout the year
Total distance	Roughly 3 miles

Agony Hill

Kip Keino

Olympic gold medalist 1,500 meters (1968), steeplechase (1972)
Ex-world-record holder 3,000 and 5,000 meters
Olympic silver medalist 5,000 meters (1968), 1,500 meters (1972)
Head of Kenyan Olympic Committee

Keino was the first of the great Kenyan runners, versatile enough to win championships at every distance from 1,500 meters through 10,000 meters. Before the 1968 Mexico City Olympics, where he would defeat Jim Ryun in an epic duel, Keino and his Olympic teammates went to a training camp at an area near Thompson Falls. There they ran three times a day. Their toughest workouts, Keino says, were long hill repeats. Runners would start out in single file up the dirt trail. They would run the repeats to the point of exhaustion.

"When I was racing, our hill workout was very important in the early stages of training, before we started doing track workouts. Near Thompson Falls we have a 1-kilometer hill we call Agony Hill, and another 2K hill in Kiganjo. It is gradual; you build up as you run up the hill. The last 100 meters you go very fast and are hurting. My record was 18 times up the hill. Then Ben Jipcho broke the record when he did it 20 times."

Kip Keino

Ryun had defeated Keino early in the winter of 1968. According to Keino, the hill repeats gave him the strength to do the very fast 200-meter intervals he realized he needed to defeat Ryun. Keino says people wanting to run hills should find a steep hill of roughly 1 kilometer, and that running it eight to 10 times is enough.

10 x 1K hill repeats

Recovery	Run down the hill
Pace	Hard
When to do	Before track training starts
Total distance	Roughly 10 miles

Fluorspar Hill

Moses Tanui

2-time Boston Marathon winner
Third-fastest marathoner ever (2:06:16)
Two-time World Championship gold medalist
Three-time World Championship silver medalist

Tanui has his own special workout called the Fluorspar Hill, a 21-kilometer climb with 23 turns that goes from the bottom of the Rift Valley to the top of its escarpment at 8,850 feet above sea level. This is the key run for scores of the best Kenyan marathoners, including 2000 Boston winner Elijah Lagat.

"I discovered this hill in 1990. Of course it is hard. It is good because it opens up your chest and it builds all the muscles at the same time. When I am training for Boston or Chicago I run Fluorspar once a week."

Moses Tanui

The runners from Tanui's training camp, called Kaptagat, gather at the base of hill very early in the morning. They start out slowly, warming up for the first mile. The runners then begin pressing the pace, past green hills with streams tumbling down the hillside. There is no traffic except herds of sheep and cows, along with an occasional mining truck. By the end of the run the group has split up, with even 2:08 marathoners dropping back. The record for the Fluorspar run is 1 hour, 21 minutes. Tanui's best on the hill is 1:24, and he often finishes behind younger, eager runners. No matter. For Tanui, it is winning races that counts, not training runs.

"One of the hardest things in training is not to rush, not to compete all the time," he explains. "My training is not to push all the time. It is to have energy for everything. There is a time to run very hard and a time to rest. Training goes together with rest."

21 kilometers uphill

Recovery	Straight uphill run
Pace	Easy at the beginning, gradually getting faster as the run progresses

The Circuit

Peter Snell

Olympic gold medal 800 meters, 1960, 1964
Olympic gold medal 1,500 meters, 1960
Ex-world-record holder, mile

The Circuit was a nearly perfect 2-mile square (perhaps just a bit short), with one-half mile segments comprising each side. Snell and the other Arthur Lydiard–trained runners in his training group ran four laps of this square, varying the speed on each side of the square.

"Others circuits were discovered (I had one on which I sustained a stress fracture of a metatarsal bone)," says Snell, "but this one was always THE Circuit."

The first half-mile was uphill. After a 3-mile warmup from Lydiard's house, Snell ran this "fairly slowly with full extension of the rear leg (for calf-muscle conditioning)." Some runners did an exaggerated "bounding" up the hill.

The next half-mile was flat and run at a relaxed pace. The third half-mile was downhill, at a grade of roughly 8 to 10 percent, and run very fast, between 1 minute 45 seconds and 1:50. "Yes, it is easy to do 1 minute 50 or better running downhill," says Snell.

The final half-mile of the Circuit was flat and again run at a relaxed pace. This section ended at the start of the uphill, where the loop was repeated. Lydiard wanted Snell to do some fast running on the two flat sides of the square, but Snell was always too "shot" to do it.

> "If you think of the total energy cost of running as being determined by stride length (thrust) and cadence (leg speed), then for a given cardiovascular stress, bounding uphill emphasizes thrust and freewheeling downhill helps develop turnover."
>
> Peter Snell

Snell did not have use of a car until he was 23, and so he sometimes ran the 5 miles from his house to the Circuit, making the warmup and warmdown a total of 10 miles.

4 x a 2-mile circuit, alternating bounding half-miles with recovery halves and fast half-miles

Recovery	Half-mile at relaxed pace
Pace	Close to race pace for the fast 880s (Snell's pace was 1:45 to 1:50)
Total distance	14 to 18 miles

6

Chapter 6

Tempo Runs: Pushing the Threshold

Tempo runs are also called *anaerobic threshold* (AT) runs. These are great for people who have a limited amount of time to train but who want to improve their racing fitness.

This workout is also known as a *sustained run*. Whatever you call it, 1993 World Championship marathon gold medalist Mark Plaatjes and University of Colorado track and cross country coach Mark Wetmore say it is an excellent way to get the most bang for your training buck, which is important for those of us who have to fit workouts in around our work schedules.

An AT workout is a steady-state run at a hard pace, anywhere from 2 to 12 miles, depending on what distance you will be racing. Unlike interval sessions, there is no break allowing you to recover from the hard running. The run is not done at race pace, but rather just below a somewhat nebulous area called your *anaerobic threshold,* the pace at which you switch from aerobic (with oxygen) respiration to anaerobic (without oxygen).

Although there are many formulas and ways to figure out your anaerobic threshold, an easy-to-remember definition used by British coach David Welch (husband of marathon great Priscilla Welch) is "your fastest sustainable pace."

"A tempo run is a very good way of getting faster without increasing the risk of injury," Plaatjes said. "In my program for the marathon the two most important workouts are the long run and the tempo run."

Wetmore, who has coached more than 70 All-Americans and is a two-time Big 12 Coach of the Year, is also a big proponent of AT runs. Says Wetmore, "The greatest training effect comes right at your anaerobic threshold. That is where you get the most stimulus for adaptation."

The nice thing about tempo runs is that they are easy to fit into your schedule, because they can be done in less than an hour. Once a week leading up to whatever race you have targeted, do a 15-minute warm-up, then run at a hard effort for 20 to 30 minutes before cooling down for 10 to 15 minutes.

"Change your shoes, do a 4-mile AT run, and you can get back to the office in time to eat a sandwich," said Wetmore. "It is a valuable workout."

Adds Plaatjes, "It is one of the most effective and efficient ways of training. You don't need a big warm-up, stretching, and strides: You just do the warm-up and the tempo run and you are done. If you do it properly you will move your lactate (the by-product of anaerobic respiration) threshold further and further, and the pace to get to your threshold gets higher and higher."

How hard should you run? Not all out, but rather at the pace at which you can no longer carry on a conversation with your running partner. The key, once again, is consistency over years, not how fast one individual AT run is done.

Many runners have a favorite loop over which they do their threshold runs, typically on dirt or the roads. Wetmore, however, often has his runners do their AT runs on the track so he can watch them and monitor their form and pace.

There is, however, a danger in doing the workout on the track—it can turn into a race instead of a training session. For example, NCAA and U.S. national 5,000-meter champion Adam Goucher completed a 5-mile AT run in 24:20 not long before winning the 1998 NCAA cross country championship. There are other runners in town who could do that run with him, but it would be a race for them while remaining a workout for Goucher. Trying to do someone else's workout usually leads to problems.

"A lot of people do their tempo run at race pace, which is not their main use. They confuse a time trial and a tempo run," said Plaatjes, who recommends tempo runs of 3 to 5 miles if you are training for a 10K.

Some coaches have their runners wear heart rate monitors set to beep once a target heart rate is exceeded. After doing AT runs for a long time, runners will likely find that they can judge what the proper pace should be. "You want to train as hard as you can within your best interpretation of your physiology and your history," says Wetmore. "You need to ask, What are the parameters for me?

"It is much better to err on the side of being 3 seconds too slow per mile than 3 seconds too fast," explains Wetmore, adding that runners should remember that their goal is to race well, not just to work out well.

Wetmore's runners wear a heart rate monitor during their AT runs, but not a watch. They will run the workout at a predetermined heart rate, such as 165 beats per minute, and will not know the time or pace per mile they were running until they finish. The most important question to ask after the run is, "Did I get the physiological workout in?"

Some days you will show up for the run with the flu, or tired from working or traveling, or it could be cold and windy, or hot and humid. No matter. Doing the workout properly means the AT run can still do exactly what you wanted it to and what you need it to do if you are to perform your best on race day.

The reason it is better to be a couple of seconds too slow per mile than too fast is that doing so takes the session from being an aerobic to an anaerobic workout. "When in doubt, back off," Wetmore says. "Here's the problem. When you move from aerobic to anaerobic, you stop the stimulus for adaptation." And the main teaching of Arthur Lydiard is that the anaerobic system adapts after 4 to 6 weeks. Doing it too soon can hurt your aerobic development, in part because it takes longer to recover from those workouts.

Track AT 10K

Alan Culpepper

> U.S. 12K national cross country champion and USATF national
>   10,000 meter champion (1999)
> Top American finisher at 1999 IAAF World Cross Country Championships
> NCAA 5,000-meter champion (1996)
> PRs: 13:28.6 (5,000 meters); 27:39.2 (10,000 meters); 3:55.1 (mile);
>   3:39.7 (1,500 meters); and 7:47.5 (3,000 meters)
> 2000 Olympic meter runner

Culpepper consistently does an AT run on the track. Culpepper and training partner Adam Goucher run 10 kilometers at 5-minute-mile pace (just over 31 minutes), wearing heart rate monitors. They keep track of their heart rates during the run, not their pace per mile. The pair do the run at the same heart rate every week; at the same heart rate, the time for the 10K decreases. It took them several years to build up to 10 kilometers.

Culpepper calls this one of his key workouts during his base phase of training, starting in the fall and going through April, when he starts doing more track-specific workouts. In college, Culpepper's AT was 5 miles. This year he and Goucher moved up to 10 kilometers for the first time, and they are running the same pace they did for 5 miles.

"I like doing the AT run on the track; that way I know how fast I need to go and can compare it to other times," says Culpepper. "Adam and I both wear heart rate monitors so we don't get carried away and run too hard. We want to keep it on the edge and stay aerobic."

Culpepper's heart rate stays at roughly 165 to 166 during this workout. "By keeping the heart rate the same we can see how we are progressing. We wear the monitor just for this workout. On other days we throw it out and just run hard. It works out pretty well."

To do this workout, you need to know your maximum heart rate. Once you know that, take about 85 percent to get your threshold. That is important, because someone could be doing an AT run at a heart rate of around 160, but he or she could be running over the anaerobic threshold.

"It is nice to use a heart rate monitor in your training, but don't become a slave to it. This workout can be done on the roads or trails. I like the track because it is safe, soft, and we can compare times and heart rates accurately. And just mentally it is easy to run on the track. It is easy for me to just click off the laps."

Alan Culpepper

Anaerobic threshold (AT) run

Recovery	No recovery during the workout
Pace	Just below your anaerobic threshold
When to do	Starting in the fall and continuing through the spring
Total distance	Anywhere from 3 to 10 kilometers

Rojas' 6K Enhanced Anaerobic Threshold Workout

Ric Rojas

Former world-record holder over 15K on the roads
New Mexico prep mile state record holder (4:11)
U.S. national cross country champion (1977)
Coach of youth and adult runners through the Ric Rojas Running Program

Rojas calls this an *enhanced anaerobic threshold workout*. You need to use a heart rate monitor for this session. First, do 15 minutes of warm-up; stretch; then do plyometrics, and finally strides. This sequence has to be followed; it is part of the workout.

Then you do an enhanced 6 kilometers on the track. The basis of the pace is your maximum heart rate. Do the first 2K at 85 percent of your max heart rate—no faster, or the workout will not work. The next 2K is run at 90 percent of your maximum heart rate, then the final 2K at 95 percent of your maximum.

> "This was not my favorite workout when I was racing; it is my favorite workout now that I am coaching. It is good because it combines a little of everything: some conditioning, some running at tempo pace, and some all-out running, all in the same workout. But it has to be structured as such."
>
> Ric Rojas

Rojas's advice is "Don't change a winning formula." He believes in planning down to the details. "You get the little stuff right, down to your heart rate per minute over your 400-meter repeats, so that you have a good foundation," he says. "What happens with some people is that they lose confidence in what they have done as they get closer to a race. A lot of people go for gimmicks, such as trying creatin, or changing their fluid replacement drink. What happens is that they read something in some pop culture magazine; some of what is written is good, but it might not be tried and true for you."

6 kilometers on the track

Pace	Based on your maximum heart rate; run the first 2K at 85 percent of your maximum heart rate, followed by 2K at 90 percent of your MHR, then a final 2K at 95 percent of your maximum
Recovery	A continuous run
When to do	All year
Total distance	8 miles

Moller's 2-Milers

Lorraine Moller

1992 Olympic marathon bronze medalist

Winner of 16 major marathons, including Boston, Osaka, and the Avon World Championships

Only person to complete the first four women's Olympic marathons

Former world-record holder, 10 miles on the track, 4 miles on the road

Coach of female marathoners

One of Moller's key workouts was 3 × 2 miles with 2-mile jog back to start.

This was Moller's favorite tempo run when she was a world-class runner, and it has now become a favorite workout of her runners.

The runners start at the base of Eldorado Springs State Park in Colorado and run out on an asphalt road for 2 miles. It has a very gradual net drop, meaning the 2-miles are run fast. With the warm-up and cool-down the workout is about 16 miles. Moller's athletes do this run every other Saturday during their buildup phase. On alternate weeks, they run a 5K tempo run.

Runners such as Melody Fairchild run the 2-miles in under 10 minutes. Moller's best average on the 2-miles was 9:16, a workout she ran before the Seoul Olympics.

"When I could run under 10 minutes on the course, I knew my leg speed was where it needed to be. This was my favorite workout, but I loved all the running I did. I loved running on the track, loved long runs, loved running with other people, and loved running by myself. I enjoyed the variety. What was key for me was understanding the purpose of the workout. If I had that understanding then the workout was valuable and fun."

Lorraine Moller

Moller likes the Eldorado Springs workout for two reasons. First, it is a beautiful run, "just so inspiring when we drive out there." Second, "it is fabulous conditioning for the marathon. The whole idea is to be at your threshold, especially when doing three of them. It is really a continuous, long workout, with some threshold work in there."

Running the workout from west to east, meaning there is a slight drop in elevation compensates somewhat for the altitude. "That way the runners can get more leg speed. But the drop is not too much, so it is not running hard downhill. It is nearly imperceptible, and gives almost a feeling of ease, of running fast."

Moller always ran this workout and her Saturday tempo runs on the same courses, week after week. She ran the 5K tempo runs not hard, "but feeling like I could keep going. If you do that and are training correctly, you should see some improvements each week. If not, you will want to cut down on some of your other runs. These Saturday runs will tell you if you are improving. If you are not, go back to your aerobic base."

A continuous run, with 3 x 2 miles

Recovery	2-mile jog back to the start
Pace	10K-race pace
When to do	During base-building phase of training
Total distance	16 miles

Oregon Sustained Run

Damien Koch

Coach of Libbie Hickman
2000 Olympic 10,000-meter runner
U.S. national 5K and 10K track champion

This workout is a regular part of Hickman's training. After a warm-up, Hickman does a steady-state continuous run of roughly 15 kilometers. She starts with 1,200 meters (three laps) on the track at 72 seconds per lap, her goal pace for 5K. Then, without stopping, she runs through the gate and off the track for 6K at her marathon race pace, between 5:30 and 5:40 per mile, on trails or a bike path. The 6K ends back at the track.

She then runs another 1,200 meters in 3:36, her 5K-goal pace, then goes off road for another 6K at marathon race pace before returning to the track and ending the workout with a very hard 1200 meters, "putting the metal to the floor."

The idea of the workout, says Koch, is to simulate what happens during a race.

"You get a little in debt at the start, then get rid of the debt while having to continue running. It helps you get used to the psychological feeling of being uncomfortable, but still being able to run without collapsing. And then you kick ass at the end. You're always recovering while under stress. And when you get into a race, you say, 'Hey, I've been here before.'"

Damien Koch

Koch picked up this workout on a 1979 trip to Eugene, where he saw Bill Dellinger coaching "a great group" that included Alberto Salazar and Matt Centrowitz. Koch modified the workout during Hickman's preparations for the Sydney Olympic 10,000 meters. After three laps on the track, Hickman ran 8 miles off road, then finished with two laps on the track, clocking 68 and 63 seconds, or 2:11 for her final 800 meters. "That's where a kick comes from," Koch said.

A 15K steady-state run, alternating three laps on the track with 6K off road

Recovery	A continuous run
Pace	The 1,200s are at 5K-goal pace; the 6Ks at current marathon race pace
Total distance	15K

The Michigan Miles

Ron Warhurst

Coach, University of Michigan

This workout is used by many athletes at different schools, often with different names and with some variations. At Dartmouth, runners knew it by then-coach Vinny Lananna's name: the Michigan workout. At North Carolina State, it was called the "Frazier" workout (for an unknown reason).

The workout starts with a mile on the track, usually at your goal race pace for 10K. For example, someone shooting for a 31-minute 10K would have a goal pace of 5 minutes. That is followed by a 1 mile recovery on the roads, at a steady pace. Next comes 1,200 meters on the track back at the original 10K goal pace (3:45 for a 31-minute 10K runner).

Next comes another 1 mile recovery on the roads at a steady pace, followed by a faster 800 meters on the track (2:20 to 2:25 for the 31-minute runner). Then comes another 1 mile recovery on the roads at a steady pace, then an all-out 400 meters.

Tom Coogan, a 29:12 10K runner, used to run this workout at Dartmouth. One day he was surprised to learn from coach Lananna that the coach didn't consider this to be a very hard workout, "but more like a secondary workout for the week or something you would do on a Tuesday or Wednesday before a race. Prior to that revelation I'd always considered it a real ball-buster," says Coogan.

The pace on the workout gets faster as the season progresses. During the cross country season, this workout can be done on a golf course.

Track and Road tempo Runs

Recovery	A continuous run consisting of a mile on the track, followed by a 1 mile recovery on the roads, 1,200 meters on the track, 1 mile recovery on the roads, 800 meters on the track, another 1 mile recovery on roads, then an all-out 400 meters
Pace	10K goal pace for harder segments, steady for the recovery segments
When to do	During racing season
Total distance	10 miles

Da Costa's 5Ks

Ronaldo Da Costa

Former marathon world-record holder (2:06:05)
Winner Berlin Marathon, Sao Silvestre 15K
PRs: 61:05 (half-marathon); 28:07.7 (10K)

Da Costa has gradually worked his way up to doing a workout of 4 ×
5,000 meters.

Da Costa's coach, Carlos Cavalheiro, is a former sprinter and now
a sprint coach who believes in faster training while maintaining fairly
high mileage. That idea paid off when Da Costa broke Belayneh
Dinsamo's marathon record at the 1998 Berlin marathon.

In this workout, all four 5Ks are 15 minutes or faster. Each gets
progressively faster, so Da Costa can get used to running quicker
when he is tired, such as happens in the second half of a marathon.
Da Costa runs between 100 and 120 miles a week, says his agent Luis
Felipe Posso, and gets strength from plyometrics.

"In marathoning, runners are increasing their cardiovascular fitness, and so
are able to keep running a good pace longer."

Felipe Posso

4 x 5 kilometers

Recovery	5 to 10 minutes between each 5K
Pace	Marathon race pace or faster
When to do	During last phase of marathon buildup
Total distance	15 to 18 miles

Mykotok's 4-Miler

Michael Mykotok

U.S. National 10,000 meter champion (1997)
PRs: 28:34.9 (10K); 48:15 (10 miles)

The workout starts with 1,200 meters (three laps) on a track at a
very fast pace. For Mykotok, this is roughly 3 minutes, 15 seconds,
which is fast enough to get into complete oxygen debt. After a 1-
minute recovery comes a 4-mile run on the track at half-marathon to
marathon pace, which for Mykotok is about 5-minute-mile pace.

This workout can help runners learn to recover from oxygen debt
and make them better able to handle the fast early pace in a race.

1,200 meters on the track, followed by a continuous 4 miles on the track

Recovery	One minute between the 3-lapper and the tempo run
Pace	Fast enough to get in oxygen debt for the 1,200; half-marathon–marathon race pace for the 4-miler
When to do	Anytime during racing season
Total distance	10 miles

10-Mile Tempo Run

Craig Young

American record holder, masters half-marathon
U.S. Master Runner of the Year, Runners World

Young sometimes ran a 10-mile tempo run after 10 miles at a decent pace. Three weeks before setting the American masters half-marathon record, Young ran the 10-mile tempo segment of this workout at 5:19-per-mile pace. The total workout was 21 miles and gave Young the confidence to go after the record, he says.

A more difficult variation of this workout is as follows: On a treadmill, start with a 3-mile warm-up. Next comes 4 miles at 19 minutes (4:45-per-mile pace) with a 1-mile jog at 6:40 pace. This is followed by another 4 miles at 19 minutes, with a 1-mile jog, then 4 miles at 19:00 with a 1-mile jog, and finally another 4 miles at 19 minutes, finishing with a mile jog.

The total distance was 23 miles, in 2 hours, 3 minutes (an average pace of 5:21 per mile). "I was pretty tired when I was done," Young says.

10 miles on road, followed by a 10-mile tempo run

Recovery	A continuous run
Pace	Medium on the first 10 miles, hard on the second 10 miles
When to do	When preparing for marathon
Total distance	21 miles

Alamosa Tempo Run

Peter De La Cerda

2nd-place finisher, 2000 Olympic trials marathon

11-time NCAA Division 2 All-American

Two-time NCAA Division 2 Champion (5,000, 10,000 meters)

PRs: 2:18:08 (marathon); 1:02:46 (half-marathon)

The workout is a 4- to 10-mile tempo run at 5-minute pace.

De La Cerda usually does the tempo runs with a group in Alamosa every weekend during the base phase of his program, sometimes every other weekend depending on how hard a week they have had. De La Cerda does the tempo runs on the road with low traffic on an out-and-back course. If there is a lot of wind, the group runs one way to let the wind carry them.

The runners do not use heart rate monitors, but they take their pulses afterward to make sure they are not running too hard. "This is a good strength workout," De La Cerda says. "It really helps doing it with a group."

As his marathon gets closer, De La Cerda will start doing a workout such as 4 × 3 kilometers in roughly 3 to 3:10 per kilometer or 6 × mile at 10K race pace. He tops off his marathon training with 20 × 400 meters in 65 to 70 seconds.

4- to 10-mile tempo run

Recovery	A continuous run
Pace	During base phase of training
When to do	When preparing for marathon
Total distance	10 to 15 miles

DeHaven's Arboretum Run

Rod DeHaven

Winner 2000 U.S. Olympic trials marathon

Winner Parkersburg (1998) and San Diego (1996) half-marathons, Park Forest
   10-miler (1998), Steamboat 4-miler (1990, 1992), Naples half-marathon (2000)

Two-time U.S. half-marathon champ (1994, 1998)

USA Running Circuit winner (1998)

PRs: 2:13:01 (marathon); 28:06.25 (10K on the track); 1:02:40 (half-marathon)

This is a 6-mile tempo run on the road, or 4-mile tempo run on the track.

For the past 8 years, DeHaven's first workout after any extended break is a tempo run. He continues running these sessions weekly for the next 6 weeks, usually on a loop through the University of Wisconsin's arboretum.

The first couple miles of the tempo run are "warm-up miles" ranging from 5:25 to 5:10. DeHaven then drops the pace on the third mile to close to 5 minutes. The last 3 miles of the run are what he calls "comfortably hard" and range from 4:55 to 4:45. DeHaven finds that the weather makes a difference on his times on the run; what is most important is not the split times but getting the effort in. "Essentially, I get 20 minutes of quality running, which I have found to be a nice strength builder," he says.

Later on in the year, during his track season, DeHaven does a similar workout, this time on the track. Once every 2 weeks, he will run 20 minutes at a predetermined pace, such as 4:45 per mile (71 seconds per lap). "If I am feeling good I try to resist the temptation of going faster than that pace."

His tempo runs give DeHaven confidence. A week before running 28:06 on the track, DeHaven ran this tempo run and easily ran 70 seconds per lap on a warm, windy day. "I was very confident heading into Harry Jerome (track meet in Canada) that I would run faster than my current PR of 28:38." And he did.

DeHaven says that average runners can incorporate a tempo run into their training by running 20 minutes at a pace slightly slower than their current 10K-race paces. Doing it on the roads or trails will work well; try it on the track if you want to closely monitor your pace, he recommends.

Those interested in looking at DeHaven's training log can check out **www.athletesvillage.com**. It dates back to July of 1999.

6-mile or 4-mile tempo run

Recovery	A continuous run
Pace	Slightly below your 10K-race pace
When to do	6-miler after resuming training after a break; 4-miler during the racing season
Total distance	10 or 8 miles

Dowling's Building Block Tempo Runs

Keith Dowling
World Cross Country team member (1994-95); Penn Relays 10,000-meter
  champion
PRs: 28:15 (10K); 2:14:30 (marathon); 3:46.4 (1,500 meters)

Dowling's tempo runs range from 4 miles to 22 miles, at a pace anywhere from 5:10 per mile for the shorter tempo runs to 5:20s for the
longer tempos.

Dowling says these kinds of tempo-threshold workouts are his favorite runs, because he feels they are "the building blocks for any
endurance athlete—at any level."

Before the 1996 Olympic trials marathon (where he placed sixth—
1 minute, 38 seconds from making the team), Dowling ran a 12-mile
tempo run at 5:15-mile pace, at the end of a 130-mile week. Running
that many miles meant he was not fresh for the workout. However,
says Dowling, "That is the key to successful marathoning: running
when you are tired. Consistency is the lethal weapon in the business
of marathoning."

The longer the distance of his tempo run, the less Dowling warms
up. For example, before a tempo run of 4 to 8 miles, Dowling warms
up 2 miles. When he does his 22-mile tempo run, however, he might
just jog a quarter-mile, to see if his shoes are fitting properly.

Dowling often does his tempo runs by himself.

"It is slightly more difficult to do any long workout alone, but that is the
point. When you are racing—you are alone."

Keith Dowling

Doing these runs alone can help you in two ways, Dowling believes:
(1) it forces you to concentrate for a prolonged period of time, and
(2) it reduces the chance of having to run someone else's pace.
"Tempo runs are based on how *you* feel, not on how your training
partner feels."

Dowling typically wears a heart rate monitor for these runs, because he knows what his anaerobic threshold is and what his heart rate should be during the session. If you do not know your threshold or what your heart rate should be in order to get the full benefit from the workout, Dowling has this advice: "For people who don't have a clue about their heart rate ranges, just run at a pace that doesn't hamper steady breathing but makes talking to your running partner (or yourself) slightly difficult."

Dowling prefers a flat course for these runs, although he will often end up on an undulating loop. He favors flat ground to make sure he can run a steady effort for the entire run. "If there are hills, I know ahead of time not to panic when I see my heart rate soar going up the hill or drop on the downhill. It is the average heart rate at the end of the workout that really matters."

No matter what the configuration of the course you run on, Dowling says to make sure not to run too fast the first few minutes of the workout. It usually takes Dowling 4 to 5 minutes to reach his target heart rate, which is slightly lower for his tempo runs over 10 miles. For example, his target heart rate for the longer runs might be 165 to 170; for tempos of less distance, the target heart rate is more like 170 to 175. Be careful not to run these sessions too hard, Dowling urges. It is better to save those efforts for race day.

Tempo-threshold run at varying distances, from 4 to 22 miles

Pace	Below anaerobic threshold
Recovery	A continuous run
When to do	Year round
Total distance	8 to 22 miles

Somers' Run of Alternating 400 Meters

Linda Somers-Smith

Olympic marathoner (1996)
Past winner of Chicago, Grandma's, Cal International, and Long Beach Marathons
Top-ranked U.S. marathoner (1995)
Marathon PR (2:30:06)

Somers said one of her toughest workouts was 2 to 3 sets of a 3-mile run. The pace for each 400 meters during the 3 miles alternates between your 5K-race pace and marathon race pace. The idea of the workout is to stay on pace until the 3 miles is complete, or as long as possible. Somers says she finished this workout "only a couple of times," and calls this the "best overall workout for a final buildup to great marathon shape. By its nature you don't have to finish it for it to have its desired effect."

This workout is done in the final phases of preparation for a marathon, and when you are in "good all-around shape," Somers says. "Otherwise, you just get trashed."

The workout can be done in different locales. Somers prefers a flat bike trail with quarter-mile segments marked off. She ran this workout alternating 76 to 77 seconds with 90-second 400 meters during each 3-mile. A month later, she did most of the workout at alternating 75 seconds with 85 seconds. "I started it once on the track, but the turns get annoying and are hard on the hips."

Somers says long runs are easier for her, which is why she likes to do the 3-milers. It helps her see if she is in shape for a race. Somers says the key to training is "putting one foot in front of the other as fast as you can for any given distance, without going over the edge on any one day or workout."

2 to 3 sets of a 3-mile run

Recovery	A continuous run
Pace	5K-race pace alternating with marathon race pace
When to do	When preparing for marathon
Total distance	10 miles

Simon Says: 10K Repeats

Lidia Simon

2:22 marathoner from Romania
Two-time bronze medalist in the World Championships marathon
Japan's Osaka Marathon winner
2000 Olympic marathoner

One of Simon's toughest workouts is 3×10 kilometer time trials on dirt roads, each one in roughly 33 minutes. Simon takes a 10-minute break between each 10K. Her coach-husband rides a bicycle alongside, giving Simon water and reading off split times. Sometimes other Romanian runners will start off with Simon, but she finishes the workout by herself.

"I like this because it helps me prepare for a marathon. I get used to running fast for a long time. Mentally, it helps during the last part of the marathon."

Lidia Simon

Runners wanting to do this workout need to work up to it over a period of years. Those preparing for their first marathon can modify the workout by doing 2×10 kilometers or 3×5 kilometers, Simon notes. "It is a hard workout to get ready for, but take your time and it will pay off."

3 x 10K

Recovery	10 minutes between each 10K
Pace	Just below race pace
When to do	Leading up to a marathon
Total distance	22 miles

7

Chapter 7

Recovery Fun: Rejuvenating With Play

I'm not sure why some of the important lessons in running are so basic, yet often so very difficult to learn. One of these simple lessons is that the benefit from training does not take place during the training, but rather while the body is recovering from the training.

How difficult can it be to recover? Very difficult for many runners, myself included. It was a lesson I did not learn in time to run my best, and which I could have learned during my first couple of runs in Boulder. The lesson was right there in front me, but I did not see it.

When I was a student at the University of Colorado, my roommate was Steve Merrill, Frank Shorter's cousin. Steve and I would at times go to Frank's house, where we would raid his refrigerator and do our laundry while he was off racing somewhere.

One day upon returning home, Shorter said, "I'm going to run. Want to join me?" "Sure," I said, excited to be running with the two-time Olympic medalist then at the height of his fitness. I threw on my shorts and we started off slowly up a slight hill. So slowly that a neighbor walking her poodle nearly kept up with us.

"Hmm, this is interesting," I thought. "I'm sure we will soon be picking it up." But we never did. We ran slowly down Fourth Street, then jogged just as slowly through campus. I remember clearly a girl from the Delta Theta sorority passing by us, wearing a big gray sweatshirt. "Dang," I thought, "I'm in better shape than I thought I was. I could easily drop Frank right now if I wanted to. But I won't; don't want to hurt his ego."

I was chomping at the bit wanting to push the pace. Such is the arrogance of youth that I really believed I was faster than Shorter. I was perhaps a 34-minute 10K runner then, while he was still in 28-minute shape. When we finished jogging our 10 miles, I said "Thanks," thinking to myself that I would have to go out later that evening in order to get in a hard run.

As I was leaving, Frank said, "By the way, I'm doing a workout tomorrow. Show up at three o'clock if you want to go."

The next day I saw that the difference between Shorter's easy days and his workout days was remarkable, as different in intensity as night and day. He and a group of elites were doing repeats on a grass field. On the first one I sprinted as fast as I could, but was dropped after the first 100 meters. I made it through the first one-lapper before having to stop, chock full of lactic acid, partway through the second. I sat on the sideline watching the group do the workout.

"A little tougher than yesterday, eh?" Shorter said with a grin and a wink when he finished.

That was one of Shorter's secrets: running his easy days very easy, and his hard days extremely hard. A simple concept, but so hard to implement for some reason. Most of us make the mistake of going medium-hard all the time. In doing so, we then become medium runners and not the champions we could be. I am reminded of the neutral angels whom Dante, that great Florentine poet, places in the first circle of Hell, because, he writes, they were neither hot nor cold. In other words, medium. In striving to run and race our best, we should sometimes be hot in our training and other times cold. Hot and cold, hard and easy, stress and recovery.

Two-time Boston Marathon winner Moses Tanui explains it like this: "One of the hardest things in training is not to rush, not to compete all the time. There is a time to run very hard and there is a time to rest."

Sometimes resting means taking a day completely off, which, unfortunately, is anathema for many runners. "It's not hard to go out and run hard," says elite runner Peter Julian. He concentrates on keeping his heart rate down on his rest days because "that's the only way to ensure you're recovering. You need to optimize your fast days, and you can't do that if your easy days are not easy. I really make sure people who want to run with me understand this. And nothing will change it. Especially with a group, it's easy to run faster than you want to."

Rob de Castella used to encounter that phenomenon among the large number of runners who came out to train with him. His way of avoiding going too fast on his recovery days was simply to turn off and take another route if a runner was pushing the pace. That meant the too-fast runner would end up either slowing down or running alone.

The purpose of recovery runs, Deek said, is "to absorb the harder sessions. So the distance and pace should be whatever it takes you to recover." The ability to run easy, he said, is just as important as the ability to run hard.

Julian agrees, saying he will see people at his recreation center trying to emulate "Rocky" every time they go out. That is the wrong approach. "Find the balance," he urges. "You must go out and enjoy the run, enjoy the scenery. Taking proper recovery days lets you do that."

Another way to keep balance and enjoyment in your training is to make a game of the run. Fun runs, even when done at a good pace, can help you enjoy your running more by giving you a mental break. I can vouch for that from my own experience with the "tube run."

On hot summer days, some of us in town will meet at Eben G. Fine Park for an easy run. Upon finishing, we jump on large, inflated inner tubes and float almost exactly a mile down Boulder Creek, tumbling over rapids and bouncing off rocks. Near the library, we get out of the water, grab the tubes, and run back up the creek on a dirt path (the record for the mile carrying an inner tube is 6:17). When we reach the park, we do it all over again. It is a pleasant way to spend an afternoon, and the cold water is good for our legs.

It is important to put fun in your running in whatever way possible. In an interview on a sports Web site, Niles West (IL) High School coach Pat Savage recounted how back in the 1960s, coach Don Amidei of DePaul University used to have his runners do something called "Lions and Tigers." During the harsh Chicago winters, the only place the coach was sure would be snowplowed was in front of the lion and tiger cages at the Lincoln Park Zoo. So that is where the team did its runs.

Now doesn't saying, "I'm going to run the Lions and Tigers this morning" sound more appealing—and heroic—than, "I'm going off to struggle through a snowdrift on the Chicago lakefront"?

Freddy's Hoof and Bike

Don "Freddy" Fredericks

Head cross country and track coach, J.D. Darnall High School, Geneseo, Illinois

The J.D. Darnall High School team always does this workout at the end of the second week of practice before school starts in the fall. The week before this bike and run, Fredericks has his runners do a steady-state run and records their times.

Based on these times, runners are paired up into two-person teams; the fastest runner with the slowest and so on until all the runners are matched up. Each team needs a bicycle and a watch.

The workout is run on a challenging 11-mile course nicknamed "the hill loop." All the teams start out together, one athlete on foot, the other on a bicycle. Every 5 minutes team members switch positions: The first runner then hops on the bike and the bicyclist starts running. This continues for the entire 11 miles.

"This is a fun run, but at the same time gives the runners an endurance workout stressing pace judgment, with the athletes running 5-minute intervals. The running part for each athlete should be done at a strong pace."

Don Fredericks

A key rule is that team members must stay together (meaning the bicyclist cannot ride ahead and leave the bike on the side of the road). The course is in the countryside, and coaches are stationed at intersections for safety. Another coach drives along with an air pump and bicycle tools.

Best of all is the awards ceremony afterward, featuring Popsicles. The winning team shares a traveling trophy. This workout is popular, with runners eager to do it before each cross country season. "It's fun for everybody," Frederick says. "The slower athletes seem to like it because they're paired up with someone they would never train with, and the faster athletes learn how to really work together even with someone who's not at the same ability level."

A series of 5 minutes of solid running alternating with biking

Recovery	5 minutes on a bicycle
Pace	Hard
Total distance	11 miles

Fun Recovery Run

Peter Julian

Pan American Games Bronze Medalist in 10,000 meters

Peter Julian says his most important run of the week is not his interval session but his recovery run. Most runners plan their week around their hard days. Not Julian. He plans his week around the days he will be recovering and builds his schedule from there. He takes 2 recovery days a week, usually Wednesdays and Saturdays, keeping his heart rate between 130 and 140. He will run anywhere from 3 to 10 miles on those days.

> "Recovery days have been the crux of my training. I really try and nail my easy days. There are lots of workouts that can get you to the top, but if you don't take an easy day, the rest of the week suffers. (British Olympian) Gary Staines told me the mistake he always sees is that people don't know how to run easy. It's hard to do."
>
> Peter Julian

It is necessary to plan your recovery days into your week in order to be consistent with them. Julian knows a month in advance which are going to be his easy days. "I don't have to wake up and think about it; I know it's coming. I think most runners are always running too hard, to be honest."

Julian says anyone wanting to be a national or world-class runner has to train hard. But it is all relative. He recommends that runners doing a couple of workouts a week should take 3 or 4 easy days in order to let their bodies rest. The reason is that "once you recover, you'll find you can attack the workouts better. Easy days can be fun; by doing them you'll find you enjoy running more instead of slogging every day."

At what pace should you do your recovery runs? Julian says to "take what you think is easy and back off 10 percent, and that should be right. On your recovery days, stay off the hills. Find an easy, flat place to run and just get into a rhythm."

Easy running

Pace	Whatever it takes to recover
When to do	Year round
Total distance	Anywhere from a complete day off to 10 miles

Running of the Dice

Aaron Berthold

Head cross country coach, Regis High School (Denver)

On a grass course in a park, set up two courses, one 600 meters long, the other 800 meters. Mark off every 100 meters with a cone. Divide the runners into groups according to ability, with three to five runners in each group. The groups are staggered so they will go off at different intervals.

The workout starts with one of the runners in the group rolling a die out of a cup. The effort the group runs depends on the roll of the die. Each number on the die, from one to six, corresponds to a workout written down by the coach beforehand.

The workout is set up like this: If a one is rolled, that group will run the whole course at a shuffle. After the first group takes off, the die is rolled again, to get the effort for the second group. If a two comes up, these runners will alternate tempo pace for 100 meters (up to the first cone) with easy pace for 100 meters (to the next cone), until they return to the start.

A roll of three means running medium pace the entire 600 or 800 meters. A roll of four is a combination of medium, easy, hard (an all-out sprint), easy, medium, hard. The coach watches to make sure his runners are accelerating when they are supposed to.

When the runners come around after their first effort, the die is rolled again. A roll of five means alternating hard, medium, hard every 100 meters. And a six means running hard the entire distance. A 600-meter course is run 10 to 12 times, an 800-meter course 6 to 8 times.

In this workout, it is not the coach telling the runners what to do, but rather the luck of the roll.

"It's fun to see what you're going to run each time around. This is not a workout to do all the time; it can be run to break up a hard day. The variety makes it fun, which is the point."

Aaron Berthold

This workout also gets the runners used to accelerating when they need to, running a hard pace, changing their pace, and learning what hard pace and medium pace mean.

Group run with frequent pace changes

Pace	Varies, from easy to all-out sprint
Recovery	Varies, depending on roll of the die
When to do	Racing season
Total distance	High schoolers will want to keep it close to their racing distance, 3 to 4 miles plus warm-up and cool-down

Kill Your Partner—If You Can

Rolando Vera

L.A. Marathon winner
2:10:02 marathoner

Silvio Guerra

Boston Marathon 2nd-place finisher
Four-time gold medalist, South American Games
Ecuadorian national record holder, every distance from 3,000 through marathon
PRs: 2:09:48 (marathon); 27:46 (10,000 meters)

This is a workout Ecuadorian runners Rolando Vera, winner of the Los Angeles marathon, and 2:09:47 marathoner Silvio Guerra used to do before Vera retired. After a warm-up, the first runner goes off hard without telling the other runners how long he or she is going to run; it might be a 30-second sprint or a 3-minute run. Then the runner slows down and recovers.

When that runner finishes it's the next runner's turn; he or she might go 1 minute hard and then rest. Then it's the next runner's turn. The pace can get very hard, Guerra explains. The idea is, "you tried to kill me, so now I try and kill you. You can play around with the time."

This workout has to be done with runners of comparable abilities. It can be run nearly anywhere: on the roads, fields, trails, or track, and with a varying number of people. If a coach is present, a variation is that he or she can decide when to stop and start the hard efforts by blowing a whistle. The runner just keeps going and going until the coach blows the whistle, at which point the next runner takes the lead.

"[During this workout] it's hard to know what to expect, which makes this similar to a race; you never know when someone is going to take off and run fast. Just like in a race."

Silvio Guerra

Group run where leader determines pace and leaders rotate

Pace	Hard efforts of varying lengths
Recovery	Varies
When to do	All year

Stinkers

Scott Winston

4:40-mile masters runner
High school coach of girls' cross country and soccer teams

This workout is a favorite of the U.S. national soccer team. It can be done at a stadium with stairs or at a flat, grassy area with a 20- to 30-meter hill nearby.

Warm up with a 1.5- to 2-mile run. Stretch well, particularly the hamstrings, quads, buttocks, calves and Achilles. Stride 5 × 75 yards. Do additional stretches between each stride if necessary.

Next set up two cones (or any object, or use the lines on a football field) 50 yards apart. Start at the first cone and sprint at 90 to 95 percent of maximum effort to the second cone. Run completely past cone number two, stop quickly and walk briskly back to it, then sprint back to the first cone. Run a total of 5 × 50 yards (which equals one "Stinker"). Note the time it took to run the Stinker, rest an equivalent time, and start again. The workout is a total of five Stinkers, or 25 × 50-yard sprints. It usually takes 50 to 60 seconds to run one Stinker, so the total drill time, including rest, is 10 minutes.

Next, rest, hydrate, and stretch for 3 to 5 minutes. During this time the coach sets up a series of 10 cones in a straight line 1 yard (roughly one walking stride) apart. Run the following circuit through the cones:

- Run through the cones stepping once between each cone and lifting the knees so that your upper leg is parallel with the ground (high stepping). Accentuate your arm swings.
- Run through the cones stepping twice between each cone (think fast feet).
- With legs together, hop over each cone (double-leg hop).
- Jump over the first five cones with your right leg and the second five cones with your left leg (single-leg hop).
- Slalom through the cones by bounding to your right through the first two cones, landing on your right foot; shifting your weight and bounding to your left through the second and third cones, landing on your left foot; shifting your weight and bounding through the third and fourth cones, landing on your right foot; and so on. Do this in one continuous motion.

Between each of the five exercises, jog back from the last cone to the first cone. Run through this circuit five to 10 times.

Rest and hydrate 2 minutes.

On a 20- to 30-yard hill, or on stadium stairs, run 20 repeats. Alternate running each repeat with either quick, small steps with knees high or longer strides with good arm swing. If no hill is available and you are running stadium stairs, alternate between running single steps (quick feet) and double steps (longer stride). Jog down to the bottom between each repeat.

Cool down with a mile run and some stretching. The purpose of this workout, explains Winston, is to develop and maintain quick leg turnover.

> "It's useful for improving a runner's start at the beginning of a race, maintaining good running form while going up hills, accelerating while passing other runners, and having a good sprint at the end of the race."
>
> Scott Winston

Masters runners whose leg speed is vanishing as quickly as their hairlines might also find the Stinkers useful, Winston says. "It's also a good mental break from the usual high miles, longer intervals, and tempo runs."

Circuit Run

Recovery	A couple of minutes between sets
Pace	A sprint
When to do	When preparing for a race
Total distance	2 kilometers

Park-to-Park Fartlek

Andy Aiken

Former coach, Nebraska Wesleyan University and Boulder (CO) High School

Get a map and find a circular route somewhere near your school, home, or wherever your workout starts. Mark off all the parks, open spaces, dirt alleys or roads, and grass stretches you can find.

Jog a mile to the first park. Stretch thoroughly and do four to six smooth, relaxed 100-meter pickups. Then, choose an appealing route through or around the park. Run your first hard effort, trying to stay smooth and relaxed and "being one with the grass," Aiken says. Then jog to another preselected park or grass stretch. Run your next hard effort, anywhere from 200 meters to a mile, before regrouping and jogging to the next park. Continue running from park to park until you have completed the required number of hard efforts. The number of hard segments will vary depending on your stage of training, Aiken says.

> "If you're in your early, buildup stage of training, make the harder stretches generally longer, with less recovery time. As you get closer to a race you're peaking for, shorten the hard stretches and increase your recovery jog."
>
> Andy Aiken

Do not time the hard efforts. Doing so, says Aiken, "defeats the purpose of getting away from the structured, timed track intervals. This is free-form, intuitive, and natural training; just go how you feel and don't worry too much about the time. Have fun, relax, and enjoy the mental break from regimented intervals."

Fartlek with breaks at parks

Recovery   Varies, depending on the distance
                  between parks

Pace   Hard

Total distance   Varies

Chapter 8

Building a Program: Preparing for Competition

When Damien Koch was competing for the University of Oregon in the late 1960s, he was inspired, like so many other runners through the years, by Emil Zatopek.

Koch read of Zatopek's remarkable training sessions, such as running in place in a tub full of laundry, bounding through the woods in Army boots, and doing huge numbers of intervals.

After finishing college, Koch wanted to be like Emil, that great humanitarian and four-time Olympic medalist known as "The Immortal Czech." So every Tuesday for 3 weeks, Koch went out and ran 80 × 400 meters. Straight through, with a 200-meter jog between each one.

"I didn't know how fast Emil had done his quarters," Koch recalls. "I just knew that this was his workout."

And what a tough workout it was. Koch would gather together 80 pebbles and pile them up, 40 at the end of the straightway on one side of the track, 40 more on the other side. After finishing each quarter, he would take a pebble from one pile and toss it aside. After jogging a half-lap recovery, he would then run his next quarter, ending up at the second pile, from which he would then toss off another pebble.

That is how Koch got through the workout; little by little the piles of pebbles got smaller. When the piles were gone, the workout was over. Counting warm-up and cool-down, it was a 30-mile session.

Being able to run 80 quarters at 72-second pace showed Koch that he was strong and fast. How did he race that summer? Not at all, because by the end of the third week he was laid up with an Achilles tendon injury.

Several years later Koch was at a reception during the New York City marathon week. His friend, the writer Kenny Moore, offered to introduce him to Zatopek, who was in town as a guest of the marathon.

"Emil," Koch said, "it's great to meet you. I did your 80-quarter workout, and I have to ask you how you were able to do that. It wiped me out."

"How fast did you run them?" Zatopek asked.

"In 72 seconds."

"Oh, that's good, that's very good," Zatopek said. "That is faster than I ran mine."

According to Koch, meeting his idol that day and talking about their shared workout made doing the 80 × 400 meters worthwhile, "even though I got injured and so burned out from it. It was stupid of me to do, but I learned a lot from it."

The key lesson Koch learned—and which all of you reading this must learn—is that simply reading or hearing about and then copying someone's workout is often not a good idea. To get the full benefit from a workout, you must modify it and adapt it to your physiology, fitness level, life situation, and training program. That is what you must do with all these workouts. Learn from them, but do not become trapped by them.

Koch went on to become a successful coach, first with Jon Sinclair, the 1983 Runner's World Road Runner of the Year, and then with two-time U.S. track champion and 2000 Olympian Libbie Hickman. Interestingly enough, Zatopek's workout so affected Koch that in his entire coaching career he has not once had his runners run a session of quarter-miles on the track.

Koch has, however, found other, better workouts, which he has passed along to his athletes. He trained with Steve Prefontaine and learned much from former Oregon coaches Bill Bowerman and Bill Dellinger, who in turn had their own influences and mentors going back decades. And now that Sinclair is coaching, the lineage continues, with those ideas getting passed along to a new crop of runners. That is how it goes in our sport; the hard-earned wisdom of the ages is codified and passed along to new-comers to running, so that they can, the hope is, avoid our predecessors' sometimes egregious mistakes. (It did take some effort to convince Sinclair that Koch really had done Zatopek's quarters. He refused to believe Koch had run that many 400s until the coach pulled out his log book from 1972 and showed him. Runners never, ever lie in their training logs, and so Sinclair was convinced.)

Like Koch, many of us want to be like the great runners. There is some-thing special about doing exactly what Zatopek, Prefontaine, or Peter Snell did in the past. It gives us a connection to these runners, even if we are not running as fast or as far as they did. In the end, what Koch learned from his experience is that he is not Emil Zatopek—nor are we. Rather, we are runners of varying abilities, talents, and potentials, and in build-ing our training programs, we must be true to ourselves.

The two best bits of wisdom I've heard that apply to training come from those great long-distance runners, the ancient Greeks ("Know thyself"), and from Shakespeare ("To thine own self be true"). Violate the first, and you may end up doing someone's else's training instead of your own, which is often a runner's tragic flaw. Violate the second, and you can end up like King Lear, wandering lost in the wilderness with only a fool for company.

By its very nature, running is an uncomplicated sport (which is per-haps why so many of us are attracted to it). The basic training ingredi-ents are simple: long runs, fast runs, slow runs, hill runs, fartlek, tempo runs, and recovery runs. It is not, however, always easy to combine these ingredients into a recipe that works for you, as Lydiard and other coaches have pointed out through the years.

What you want to do in your schedule is mix the ingredients to give you these components, which are the key elements in any training pro-gram: muscular and skeletal strength; speed and endurance; pure speed, and recovery.

Building your own program is more difficult than it might appear on paper. I call it *your own training program* because even if you get a work-out or workouts from someone else, you must modify them to suit your own tastes. A workout that sounds good might not be what you need at all. Running Adam Goucher's or Alan Culpepper's 500-meter intervals might sound appealing, but it could be the wrong training for you.

What is more important is exposing yourself to new ideas and gleaning the important principles from them. Keeping all this in mind, here are some rules I've found valuable through 25 years of long-distance running: train smarter, not harder; build a foundation; run with friends; choose your workouts carefully; pick out target races; take a taper; and undertrain.

Train Smarter, Not Harder

The hallmark of successful runners, no matter what level, is consistency. In putting together your training program, you must look long term. That is sometimes hard to do in our harried, 24-7 Internet world where we have instant access to nearly everything. Success in long-distance running, however, is anti-instant access. It comes from inexorably doing your running and steadily, little by little, getting fitter and stronger.

I've known many runners who've come to town and done great training for a month or two with some of the local elites before vanishing without a trace. They don't last because they get injured or lose interest. Without consistency, even the best-laid plans of runners go astray. That is why the first rule to keep in mind when you're deciding which workouts to run should be that the session "do no harm." That way you will be able to keep your running going and reach your goals.

What is the best training program? The one that works for you. There are many ways to train, but there are also just as many—or more—incorrect ways of training. Running as hard as you can as often as possible will get you fitter faster but will also increase the possibility that you will be left battered and broken down by the side of the track.

All of you reading this book have the motivation to train. Without that motivation, that will to persevere, all the words written in books, in magazines, and on the Internet are mere theories floating around in the ozone. Most likely you are like Koch: You have a superabundance of energy and a strong work ethic (otherwise you'd be sitting on the couch watching the Jerry Springer show instead of trying to figure out how to train).

The question then becomes, "How is that motivation directed?"

In Koch's case, it was misdirected, as it is for so many of us. That is because we runners can be—this is something we are not ashamed to admit among ourselves—a bit compulsive at times, meaning we run the risk of pushing ourselves past our limits.

Compare Koch's session with Rob de Castella's 8 × 400 meters. Deek, whom most would consider one of the greatest marathoners ever, never ran more than eight 400s on the track at one time. He could, of course, have done scores more, but it was more important for him to run his workouts consistently week after week, year after year, than to run as many 400s as fast as he could in any one particular session. It was the cumulative effect of his workouts over years, starting when he was a teenager, that made Deek a champion.

There is a valuable lesson in comparing these two runners. Rather than making each workout as difficult as possible, being motivated means training as consistently as you can for as long as you can, pushing yourself to the edge on your workout days without going over that edge. Knowing all the greatest workouts in the world will do you no good if you have gone a step too fast or too far and gotten hurt.

Deek often used to put it this way when speaking with the many nascent runners who flocked to his doorstep seeking advice: "Train smarter, not harder."

Training smarter will give you gradual improvement and will, explains Shaun Creighton, allow you to adapt to and absorb your training. "You'll improve every year, and you'll enjoy it more."

And enjoying your running, even while working hard when it is time to work hard, means you will be more likely to keep your training going. Longevity is what running is all about, whether you are training to break a world record or to finish your first marathon. The proper program for you is one that gives you satisfaction and enjoyment in all aspects of your training, from easy runs to hard workouts.

My rough estimate is that 95 percent of the runners I know do not train properly (I count myself among them, unfortunately). The mistakes are numerous, yet easy to avoid. Stay healthy and train smart, keep plugging away, do good workouts and recover from them, and you will improve. Guaranteed. That is the great thing about our sport.

Build a Solid Aerobic Foundation

Former NCAA 1500-meter champ Steve Holman compares formulating a training program to building a house: "You can't start right away with speedwork; that would be like moving the furniture in before putting the roof on. You have to have a good foundation and follow the plan in the correct order."

Holman is one of many top runners who have come to this realization. When Peter Snell defeated world-record holder Roger Moens in winning the gold medal in the 1960 Rome Olympic 800 meters, the key, Snell said, was the weekly 22-mile runs he had done in the Waiatarua Hills. Snell slowly built up his endurance as the foundation for later developing his speed.

Your training program, for any distance from 800 meters on up, has to start with a commitment to developing a good foundation. This phase is usually done during the winter months, when there are not many races available. It involves steady aerobic running, anchored by one long run, or even two, if you are experienced enough and are training for a marathon.

The total volume should be increased gradually, until you reach a level that you can handle within the constraints of work and family life. For elite runners, this typically goes up to 120 miles a week; other people serious about their training should be able to handle a minimum of 50 miles a week.

You do all this aerobic stimulation to get to the point at which you are now ready to train. This is one of the basic principles successful runners live by—build a substantial aerobic foundation before moving on to your workouts.

I like the way Lorraine Moller explains the need for a base: "Training for a race is like building a bank account with aerobic credits: the more aerobic credits you build up, the more you have to spend. Then the way you spend those credits is by doing anaerobic work. It can be a good or a bad investment, depending on your recovery [from the workout]."

The two keys to building your base are these:

- Time on your feet is more important than distance.
- Do your aerobic running at a pace that allows you to "absorb" the running and doesn't leave you flattened.

You will want to run steady on your aerobic runs, but for most of us, the pace does not matter as much as the length of time we are out there. A good guide, says coach Rich Castro, is doubling your resting heart rate on your aerobic runs. Try to get with a big gang on a Sunday morning, and go at a pace where you can talk all the way. These aerobic runs should not leave you "just hanging on with your eyeballs falling out," as Steve Jones so colorfully puts it.

You can do your aerobic runs too fast. What happens then is that you often begin rationalizing why you are cutting a run short. There is, however, no rationalization in long-distance running; there are only hard-earned, sound physiological principles that coaches and runners have learned over the years.

And the soundest principle of all is getting in as much aerobic stimulation as possible before doing your anaerobic workouts. As Lydiard puts it, "Your aerobic capacity is almost infinitely trainable."

I saw the importance of having a good base in the spring of 2000 with Adam Goucher. In February, he won both the 4K and the 12K U.S. national cross country championships. Soon afterward, however, he hurt his Achilles tendon. Then, after 8 full weeks without running a step, Goucher was finally healthy again. His first workout when he resumed training was a 4-mile AT run on the track (as explained in chapter 6).

Keeping his heart rate at 168 beats per minute, Goucher ran the 4 miles at 5:12-per-mile pace. Three weeks later, he did another AT run. Once again keeping his heart rate at the same 168 beats per minute, Goucher ran 6 miles in 29:20—a huge improvement of 4:57 per mile, yet at the same effort. He was able to do this because of the deep aerobic base he had built up through months of 100-plus mile weeks, capped by regular 20-mile runs on Magnolia Road (see chapter 1).

Trying to run speedwork without a base can only—sometimes sooner, sometimes later—lead to disaster. Building a strong aerobic base increases your body's ability to supply oxygen to the muscles by increasing the blood vascularization of the muscles, while at the same time improving your neuromuscular efficiency. This is the beginning of the path to running well.

Run With friends

Having company when you run is critical for consistency, which, as I noted before, is the linchpin of long-term success. Running is often difficult, and going with friends makes the time more enjoyable, even on a long run or a workout.

"The group effect is very important," says Peter Snell, who won three Olympic gold medals for New Zealand. "When I started training with Arthur [Lydiard], he put me in with runners who wouldn't do a number on me. I ran at a pace I could handle, which was a nice introduction to becoming a long-distance runner. There are a lot of people with huge talent out there, but they are too competitive in training, and their talent just gets trained out of them."

De Castella used to run with people of all abilities and fitness levels, from freshmen in high school to world-record holders. Running with a group gave Deek and the rest of us stability in our training programs, because it made us accountable for showing up for a workout at a certain time on a certain day. Some days you will feel good on the runs, some days bad; it doesn't matter as long as you are getting out the door every day. Good training partners can help you do that.

Another key point: make your runs with friends fun whenever possible. Training does not have to be all drudgery and hard work. One Sunday when I was going to cover a road race in a nearby town for the newspaper, I decided to run to the race with Steve Jones. We ran on a "secret" trail through the mountains west of town that I thought I remembered from past runs. It turned out I did not remember it very well, and all the valleys, junipers, and cacti looked the same. We lost the trail and had to run cross country to get to the race, jumping across gullies and over deer bones picked clean by coyotes and mountain lions.

"This trail is so secret the animals don't even know about it," Jones said as he pulled cactus needles out of his shoes. We struggled in and had to walk the last hot mile down a highway into town. By the time we got there, exhausted, the race was over, with only some oranges and a few drinks left. We caught a ride back home, and as he left, Jones turned and said, "Hey, that was a great run. Thanks. Same time next week?"

Enjoying his sport is what running is all about for Jonesy, even if it means getting lost now and then.

If you don't know any runners in your town, join a group. Every city has its runners, battle-scarred veterans of countless road and track races. Go on runs with them and they will likely be glad to take you under their wings.

Choose Your Workouts Carefully

You have your base. You have some training partners to run with. Now what? Your training schedule should incorporate the following elements.

- A period of winter base building (see chapter 1).
- A period of building speed and endurance while continuing to do your aerobic base runs (see chapters 2-6). This involves one to three workouts per week, depending on your fitness and strength and the time of year.
- A period of speedwork (see chapters 2, 3, and 4).
- A focus on making sure you are recovered from your weekly workouts (see chapter 7).
- And finally, a taper leading up to a race.

You can use the same principles the elites do, although the amount and intensity of your training will be less. Many runners like to run their workouts on the same days every week. Do that and it will give your training, and your life, a structure and continuity that make it easier to keep running.

Some runners, such as de Castella and Steve Moneghetti, ran the same workouts 52 weeks a year. The emphasis varied depending on the time of year and the races they were training for. Australian coach Pat Clohessey calls this "complex training," not because it is difficult to understand, but because it incorporates all aspects of running—hills, tempo runs, intervals, long runs—into 1 week.

Other runners, like Creighton, Steve Jones, and Rosa Mota, employ the same principles year after year, but not necessarily the same workouts. In the weekly training schedules that follow, I'll give you some sample schedules; it's up to you to pick the workouts that best suit your personality, to choose the ingredients for the "cake" you want to bake.

You might find one or two workouts you like and stick with those; that was my approach when I was running my best. Or, you might be the kind of runner who wants to vary your workouts week to week. If so, you have a variety to choose from in this book. Be realistic. Don't draw up a schedule of workouts that look great on paper but that you won't be able to handle.

Which workout should you do on Tuesday, and which on Thursday or Friday? Go through the workouts in this book, and try to find ones that are appealing. You will have to modify them to suit your fitness and strength.

You will find out soon enough—perhaps in the middle of an interval session—whether a workout is for you. If you walk away from the workout, or to the workout, wishing you were going to do something else, you probably should be doing that something else, whether it's swimming, mountain biking, or walking.

However, if you walk away from the workout feeling tired, but at the same time glowing with the satisfaction that comes from a job well done, then you know this is a workout for you. And when you just can't wait until your next workout, then you really know you are on the right track.

I have found that the simplest training schedules often work the best. For a couple of years I trained with English runner Mark Scrutton. Scrutton, who won the NCAA cross country championship and broke 28 minutes for 10K, ran only two different workouts during his 4 years in college: an anaerobic threshold run (which he called a "sustained run") and a set of 200-meter intervals, with a fast float for a recovery.

The progression in Scrutton's training went like this: In the winter, he would run three sustaineds a week, in snow with sweats, not worrying about the time. In the early spring, the weekly schedule changed to two sustaineds and one 200 session. In late spring, he cut out one sustained run and added another set of intervals. Finally, when peaking for the NCAAs, Scrutton ran three fast 200-meter interval sessions a week.

Two workouts, two NCAA titles. The ingredients were simple, and the recipe worked. Once he found his program, Scrutton did not change his training or jump from one coach to another.

When doing workouts, I sometimes am reminded of the day I was down at the track, where an NCAA All-American was running 400-meter repeats. Frank Shorter, who was watching, shook his head and said, "He'll never be a great runner."

"How can you tell from watching just one interval session?" I asked.

"Look, you see, at the end of the 400 he doesn't run all the way through. He stops a step short of the line."

For Shorter, not following all the way through on the interval meant the runner was not following through on the training. And he was right. That runner quit training soon after college.

Pick Target Races

The best way to build a training schedule is to pick out a race and then work backward 6 to 8 weeks. Why 6 to 8 weeks? Because that's the amount of time Lydiard and others say is required to build your anaerobic system. According to Lydiard, a well-conditioned runner (one with a good aerobic base) can reach a peak quickly, sometimes in as little time as 4 weeks.

Someone might ask you the question, Why race at all? Why not just run, staying fit and in shape? The answer is that racing is the whetstone that sharpens your will to run. It gives you a reason to do the workouts, to make a plan and to stick to it. Racing is the test that proves your fitness. It's the goal that gives an edge to your training, the end that justifies the means, and the way you test yourself (not just against others, but against yourself).

Picking a race is important because it gives you something to aim for during the long weeks of training, something to build and focus on. Otherwise your running can get "aimless and desultory," as Richard Benyo, editor of the magazine *Marathon & Beyond,* explains it.

Pick out one key race in the late spring or early summer, and another in the fall. You will likely run some races in between, but those can be low-key races that bookend the two you are peaking for. Use early-season races as a goal to build up your spring training as you come out of the winter doldrums.

Running a variety of races can help you build a love of running, "as opposed to just jumping into a marathon—and falling out the other side," says Benyo. By that, he means that some people enter one race, finish it, and then quit running entirely. It's much better to have a lifetime of running.

Most of you are probably familiar with that ineffable glow you get from challenging yourself and racing well, when you have pushed yourself as hard as you can. And isn't that what running is all about in the end, challenging ourselves?

I had that thought last summer when I was up in Steamboat Springs for a road 10K at 8,000 feet. It was a small field of several hundred people. After the first steep hill, I found myself running with Arturo Barrios and some of his Army runners. They were doing the race as a tempo run, monitoring their heart rates. I, however, was racing, pushing myself as hard as I could. Coming down a hill at 2-1/2 miles, I passed Barrios. For the first time ever, I was ahead of the former 10K world-record holder.

Glancing to the side, I could see by his shadow that he had dropped back a step or two. Adrenaline rushed through my body and jumped on my red blood cells. I surged, watching his shadow fall farther behind me. I was pulling away and running strong.

A half-mile later, however, Barrios and his runners passed me up a gradual incline, and I could not hang with them. I ended up pulling out at 5 miles because of a twinge in my calf, but how exciting it was to be racing Barrios. I was encouraged by the effort, and that feeling of leading him fueled my training for the rest of the summer.

Since then, I have picked out the local race where I aim to beat him in 2001. That's my motivation to still train seriously and do the best workouts I can: to get fit enough to beat Barrios, Jones, Austrian journalist Knut Okresek, and a few others in a race. I will never reach my personal bests again, but I can still dream of beating my rivals. That's what fuels my training.

Take a Taper

You've done the training and are now ready to race. That means it's time to back off and begin what is called a *taper*. This is a period of lower mileage that allows your body to recover from the past months' training and enter your target race fresh and ready to roll.

Many coaches and elites say that it's critical to taper. Otherwise a runner can go into a race fatigued. "I see it all the time," says Lorraine Moller. "It's the most common mistake runners make."

When doing your taper, use the following guidelines:

- Don't change your training leading up to the race.
- Starting 2 weeks before the race, cut out your long run.
- Do a shorter version of your regular Tuesday workout the week of the race.
- Starting the Thursday before your race, don't do any hard running.
- Take a complete rest day—no running at all—a day or two before the race. Or just do some easy running.
- Run 6 to 10 strides a bit quicker than race pace 2 days before the race.

Barrios used to cut his mileage down about 30 percent so that he always felt rested going into a race. Shorter did not cut back much the weeks before he won his Olympic medals in 1972 and 1976 because, he said, "I would get too nervous."

Bobby McGee, coach of South African Olympian Colleen De Reuck, says runners should aim to go into a race feeling "crisp and brisk."

On race day, you are on your own. "This is not like basketball or baseball, where even if you are not 100 percent, your teammates will help you out and you can still win," says Barrios. "In a race, it's only you against the clock, and there will not be anybody to stop the clock, stop the race, or call a time-out. It's you against everybody."

Don't be one of those many runners who leave their races in their workouts. You know these runners, the kind who are always making excuses for a poor race. "Most people do not realize their potential when racing because they aren't doing the right training," says Barrios. "You don't want to go into the race thinking you're ready when you're not."

Undertrain

As you put your program together and are anxious to push yourself in your training, consider the following advice from de Castella and Ingrid Kristiansen. One morning after a group run, I asked Deek and Ingrid what the secret to running well was. Surprisingly, both told me their secret was undertraining.

At first I thought they were joking, but Deek and Ingrid, though fun-loving, were always serious when talking about training. What the two meant was that they often finished a run feeling they could have run faster, or longer. The point is that it's better to be 10 percent undertrained than 1 percent overtrained. That allows you to stay on top of your running and not get injured.

Many runners have what de Castella calls the "foolish idea" that if they do a little more, and faster, they will get better. This, says Deek, "ignores the fact that you must train at your *optimal* level, not your *maximum* level."

When doing your running, try to think of gradually adapting to the training within your body's current level of strength and fitness.

There is a wide range of workouts presented here. You can look through, modify, and use the programs that follow. Make sure you consider the following four ingredients when you plan your training:

- Strength, which you get through the long runs in chapter 1, the fartlek in chapter 5, and the hills in chapter 6.
- Speed and endurance, which you get from longer intervals, repeats, and fartlek.
- Pure speed, from the shorter, faster intervals.
- Recovery, so that you absorb the training, because the training benefit comes when you rest. You don't want to run so hard that you get injured or can't recover, but you need to run hard enough to get the training stimulus.

I noticed that Amy Skieresz, who won seven NCAA titles at the University of Arizona, recently announced she was retiring at age 23. Skieresz is the only woman to win NCAA cross country, indoor 5,000 meters, outdoor 5,000 meters, and 10,000 meters in one school year. Without a doubt, her best years were ahead of her. Unfortunately, it appears she will join the ranks of talented, fast American runners who got out of the sport early.

Those runners who will be running in the 2004 and 2008 Olympics will not necessarily be the most talented ones, but rather those who are able to stick with their running long enough to develop their potential. That means backing off from the maximum amount of running you can do and finding your optimum training schedule.

I hope you are one of those runners who will stick with it for a lifetime. If so, you will not want to let your running take over your life. Even a winner of multiple world records like Kristiansen did not pay attention to running when she was not training. She took care of her family, knitted, read, and took classes.

Collen De Reuck is the same way: "Balance your running and your life. Have other priorities. See beyond your next race," De Reuck says, urging runners to most of all "enjoy your sport."

Do that, and you'll have a chance of becoming the runner you were meant to be. How far will that take you? Hard to say, but when talking to young runners, I always give them Arthur Lydiard's explanation as to how he found three Olympic medalists within a short radius of his Auckland home: "There are champions everywhere."

Could you be one of them? It's nice to think so, isn't it?

5K Training Program

If your target race is a 5K, a distance that is becoming more and more popular, your base, or foundational work, will be similar to that for a 10K. This base period should be done for as long as possible, and in any case should last a minimum of 3 months. During this time you will be focusing on your steady long runs and AT workouts from chapter 6, or longer fartlek or grass repeats (chapters 2 and 3).

If you plan on running only 5Ks during the year, and no 10Ks or marathons, your base work can comprise roughly 10 percent less total volume than if you were training for longer races.

Runners training for a shorter race like a 5K sometimes ask why they need to run aerobic distance; why not just run fast all year long? Again, the reason is based on sound physiological principles.

- The anaerobic foundational work you do in your base phase builds up your cardiovascular *delivery system*.

- The anaerobic workouts you do once you are strong enough to handle the faster running develop your cardiovascular *pumping system*. It does no good to have a great pumping system if your body is unable to transport blood to your cells.

Once your delivery system—the myriad capillaries and other blood vessels developed through the aerobic base work—is at a high level, then you can do 6 to 8 weeks of specific training for your 5K. When you start this training you will, however, want to make a few adjustments from your 10K schedule.

First, your longer speed and endurance workout on Tuesdays will be done at your 5K goal pace. For example, if your goal is to run 15 minutes, 30 seconds for the race, a typical Tuesday workout (on the grass, roads, or track) might be repeat half-miles in 2 minutes, 30 seconds.

If your goal pace is 6-minute miles (18:38 for 5K), the half-miles would be run in 3 minutes. The same workout for a 17:05-minute 5K runner (5:30 per mile) would be 2:45 per half. The recovery will be whatever is needed to keep the half-miles at your goal pace.

Second, the big difference comes on your second workout of the week. This will be a pure speed workout, geared toward what a miler would do. An example of this workout is fast 400-meter repeats with a longer recovery.

If you are choosing workouts from chapters 2 or 3 for your second workout of the week, you will be running more by effort than by the stopwatch. In this case, the difference from your 10K training is that you will be doing more 30-second to 1-minute repeats, rather than short interval sessions on the track.

You can race 5Ks year round, as long you know that most of the races will be run when your legs and body are fatigued. Use these races as part of your training, to get used to having to run hard when you are tired. Then there will be those couple of races each year that you peak for, when you want to run your personal record. Those races will be preceded by a taper.

A run that British runners, among them Welsh former marathon and half-marathon world-record holder Steve Jones, use to develop their speed without a great deal of stress is called the *acceleration run.* This run is similar to what runners in the United States might know as a *pickup,* and it can be a valuable addition to your 5K training schedule.

If you are strong enough, you can do the accel run in the afternoon after one of your recovery runs. Find a grass field and mark it off with cones, hats, or T-shirts, every 35 meters (this is easy to do if you can get permission to run on a football field).

Run the first 35 meters steady, accelerate in the next 35-meter segment, and then wind down on the last 35 meters. If you're on a football field, take a short jog across the end zone to the next sideline, and do another accel run. If you're on an open grass field, just take a 20- to 30-second jog.

Start with no more than four (two laps of the football field) of these accel runs. Eventually, you can work your way up to doing 12 laps of accels, as Jones used to do. In addition to strengthening your hips, glutes, and quadriceps, these accels are a great way to work on changing your pace while running, says Jones. "They teach you how to accelerate when you're racing. I'm seeing that now more than ever before."

As with the 10K schedule, in this program you'll run one longer workout and one shorter workout each week. And as with a 10K, those of you who want to run 9-minute-mile pace (27:56 for the 5K) should not worry about workouts right now. Instead, just go out and run steady several times a week. Try going over a variety of terrain so that you start to get stronger by running up and down hills. Taking a walking break is fine. Keep your running going consistently, and you'll be surprised how aerobically fit you'll become.

Table 8.1

5K Schedule

	Daily Workouts	Special Considerations
Week 1	**Monday:** Recovery 40 minutes to 1 hour of easy to solid running, depending on how you feel **Tuesday:** Speed and endurance workout (chaps. 2-6), such as 4 × 5 minutes hard **Wednesday:** Recovery **Thursday:** Recovery followed by acceleration runs **Friday:** Speed workout (chaps. 2-4), such as 10 × 1 minute on the grass **Saturday:** Recovery 40 minutes to 1 hour **Sunday:** Long run 1:15 to 2 hours	An easy way to increase your volume of training is to add in a second run several times a week. This can be as little as 30 minutes or as much as 75 minutes. If you feel fatigued at the start of most of your runs, cut back on this second run until you feel on top of your training again.
Week 2	**Monday:** Recovery 40 minutes to 1 hour of easy to solid running **Tuesday:** Speed and endurance workout (chaps. 2-6) **Wednesday:** Recovery followed by acceleration runs **Thursday:** Recovery **Friday:** Speed workout (chaps. 2-4) **Saturday:** Recovery 40 minutes to 1 hour **Sunday:** Long run 1:15 to 2 hours	Make a concerted effort to recover from the hard sessions. Always keep in mind that you get the benefit from training not while doing the actual workout, but when you rest. There is no training benefit without recovery, the time we give the body to repair and rebuild itself.
Week 3	**Monday:** Recovery 40 minutes to 1 hour of easy to solid running **Tuesday:** Speed and endurance workout (chaps. 2-6), such as 1K repeats **Wednesday:** Recovery followed by acceleration runs **Thursday:** Recovery **Friday:** Speed workout (chaps. 2-5), such as 10 × 500 meters **Saturday:** Recovery 40 minutes to 1 hour **Sunday:** Long run 1:15 to 2 hours	The danger in specific 5K training is that by doing faster speed workouts once a week, you increase your chance of injury. This is because of the greater stress on your joints, tendons, and ligaments. Always back off any time you feel a twinge in your muscles or joints. This is hard to do; having a coach as a sounding board can really help.

Table **8.1**

	Daily Workouts	Special Considerations
Week 4	**Monday:** Recovery 40 minutes to 1 hour of easy to solid running **Tuesday:** Speed and endurance workout (chaps. 2-6) **Wednesday:** Recovery followed by acceleration runs **Thursday:** Recovery **Friday:** Speed workout (chaps. 2-4) **Saturday:** Recovery 40 minutes to 1 hour **Sunday:** Long run 1:15 minutes to 2 hours	Here is Frank Shorter's advice on getting the most out of your training: "On your hard days go as hard as you can. The other days obey your instincts—you can do as little as you want and as slowly as you want as long as you are out there for at least a half hour. Chances are you will want to do more, but always make it easy."
Week 5	**Monday:** Recovery 40 minutes to 1 hour of easy to solid running **Tuesday:** Speed and endurance workout (chaps. 2-6) **Wednesday:** Recovery followed by acceleration runs **Thursday:** Recovery **Friday:** Speed workout (chaps. 2-4) **Saturday:** Recovery 40 minutes to 1 hour **Sunday:** Long run 1:15 to 1:30	Begin cutting back on your long run, especially if your legs are tired from some of the fast workouts. Stop at 1 hour, 30 minutes for the next 2 weeks, then run 1:15 on your long runs the following 2 weeks. Do not do a long run the week of your race.
Week 6	**Monday:** Recovery 40 minutes to 1 hour of easy to solid running **Tuesday:** Speed and endurance workout (chaps. 2-6), such as repeat half-miles **Wednesday:** Recovery followed by acceleration runs **Thursday:** Recovery **Friday:** Speed workout (chaps. 2-4) **Saturday:** Recovery 40 minutes to 1 hour **Sunday:** Long run 1:15 to 1:30	This week you'll do some sharpening workouts, such as a 200-300-400-600 ladder, or 200-meter intervals. Start taking more recovery between your hard efforts in order to run them at a faster pace.

(continued)

Table **8**.**1** *(continued)*

5K Schedule

	Daily Workouts	Special Considerations
Week 7	**Monday:** Recovery 40 minutes to 1 hour of easy to solid running **Tuesday:** Speed workout **Wednesday:** Recovery followed by acceleration runs **Thursday:** Recovery **Friday:** Speed workout (chaps. 2-4), such as 10 × 300 meters **Saturday:** Recovery 40 minutes to 1 hour **Sunday:** Long run 1:15	Think about where you're going to be racing. If it's a local race, run the course early in the morning this week before traffic starts. Remember the key points along the route; if there's a hill, do some hill sprints this week. When you're hurting during your intervals in training this week, pretend you're on the last 400 meters of your race. Relax and concentrate on keeping good form.
Week 8	**Monday:** Recovery 40 minutes to 1 hour of easy to solid running **Tuesday:** Speed workout **Wednesday:** Recovery followed by acceleration runs **Thursday:** Recovery **Friday:** Speed workout **Saturday:** Recovery 40 minutes to 1 hour **Sunday:** Long run 1:15	This week, you'll do two speed workouts as you try to put the finishing touches on your training. A nice way to get in some leg turnover is through a workout called "straights and turns." After a warm-up and strides, run the straightaways on the track hard, and "float" the turns at a steady pace. Do 2 to 3 miles of that this week on Tuesday, followed by a fast speed workout later in the week.
Week 9	**Monday:** Recovery 40 minutes **Tuesday:** Reduced speed workout **Wednesday:** Recovery followed by acceleration runs **Thursday:** Recovery **Friday:** Rest day **Saturday:** Easy jog **Sunday:** Race	This is your taper week. Cut back on your Tuesday hard workout. If you have 8 × 400 meters planned, reduce it to four or six 400s at 80 to 85 percent of your goal race pace. Remember that nothing you do this week is going to help you for your race; you can, however, do much that will hurt you come race day. If you have difficulty cutting back, do some easy accel runs Wednesday and Thursday. This can help your mental state.

10K Training Program

After setting the world marathon record back in 1984, Steve Jones was asked if he now considered himself a marathon runner, a track runner, a cross country runner, or a road racer. Jonesy's simple reply? "I'm a runner."

That is perhaps the best attitude to take when laying out and following through on your training program. All the training you do is related; when you train for a 10K you are also preparing for 5Ks, half-marathons and marathons. There is often a correlation between a runner's 10K time and his or her marathon time, and also with their races over shorter distances.

In this program, as with your 5K training, you will run one longer workout and one shorter workout each week, in addition to your long run. The longer interval or anaerobic threshold workout is on Tuesday; your second weekly workout will be something shorter and faster, either on Thursday or Friday. There will be a little more emphasis on endurance in your 10K training as well as a bit more volume. However, this is done without sacrificing your "pure speed."

When looking back in this book for workouts to do in getting ready for your 10K, you will likely want to modify the sessions by changing the target pace to correspond to your goal. At the beginning of your racing season, after doing your base phase of training, you might want to start out taking longer recoveries and running fewer reps. For example, when doing Rob de Castella's 400-meter interval workout, you can start out with five 400 meters and work your way up to eight.

As your training progresses, you will find the workouts that suit your fancy—your own "money workouts" that you just know are going to get you in peak fitness for your 10K. Experiment on your hard days until you find the workouts you like best. And, remember what Peter Tegen, coach of Suzy Favor Hamilton, says: "It takes courage to rest." That means when you feel a slight injury coming on, or are feeling overly cranky or fatigued, take the day off. The smart runner is the one who survives to train another day. This is important because you want to make sure you are getting the benefit from all your workouts, both physically and mentally. That way when you line up for your target 10K, you can be confident you have done the work necessary to run your best.

When following your 10K schedule, remember that you are different from any other runner. As much as possible, try and understand the theory that underlies your training, so that you are not just haphazardly taking a workout out of context.

In the following table I've listed three time goals. For those of you not aiming for a specific time for the 10K, your best bet is to simply go out and alternate running and walking several times a week. As you get stronger, you will want to start running faster; that is the time to start doing workouts.

Table 8.2

10K Schedule

	Time Goals and Daily Workouts	Special Considerations
Week 1	***32 to 40 minutes*** **Monday:** Recovery 1 hour to 1:15 **Tuesday:** Plasencia mile workout (chap. 2) 5 × 1 mile (5:30) **Wednesday:** Recovery 1 hour to 1:15 **Thursday:** Recovery 1 hour **Friday:** Grass repeats (chap. 2) 8 × 1 minute **Saturday:** Recovery 50 minutes easy **Sunday:** Long run 1:30 to 2 hours ***40 to 50 minutes*** **Monday:** 40 minutes easy **Tuesday:** 4 × 1 mile (6:30) **Wednesday:** 40 minutes easy **Thursday:** 40 minutes easy **Friday:** 6 × 1 minute **Saturday:** 45 minutes easy **Sunday:** Long run 1:15 ***50 to 60 minutes*** **Monday:** 30 minutes easy **Tuesday:** 3 × mile (7:30) **Wednesday:** 30 minutes easy **Thursday:** 30 minutes easy **Friday:** 4 × 1 minute **Saturday:** 40 minutes easy **Sunday:** Long run 50 minutes	Don't eschew stretching. An easy way to get a consistent stretch in every week is by taking a yoga class. Don't be intimidated by people in class who can put their legs around their heads and balance on one finger; you most likely will be able to run circles around them on the track. Don't compete with others while stretching in a class; save that for your race. Instead, pay attention to your body and your breathing. When you can focus and concentrate on a stretch for a period, not finding it too hard or too boring, you know you are doing it properly.

Table **8.2**

	Time Goals and Daily Workouts	Special Considerations
Week 2	**32 to 40 minutes** **Monday:** Recovery 1 hour to 1:15 **Tuesday:** Culpepper anaerobic threshold run (chap. 6) 20 minutes at a heart rate just below threshold **Wednesday:** Recovery 1 hour to 1:15 **Thursday:** Recovery 1 hour **Friday:** Grass repeats (chap. 2) 10 × 30 seconds **Saturday:** Recovery 50 minutes easy **Sunday:** Long run 1:20 **40 to 50 minutes** **Monday:** 40 minutes easy **Tuesday:** 15 minutes **Wednesday:** 40 minutes easy **Thursday:** 40 minutes easy **Friday:** 8 × 30 seconds **Saturday:** 45 minutes easy **Sunday:** Long run 1:15 **50 to 60 minutes** **Monday:** 30 minutes easy **Tuesday:** 10 minutes **Wednesday:** 30 minutes easy **Thursday:** 30 minutes easy **Friday:** 6 × 30 seconds **Saturday:** 40 minutes easy **Sunday:** 50 minutes	At this point you can still be increasing your weekly mileage, as long as you're able to handle the increased volume. You can do it through a second run or by increasing the length of your runs on nonworkout days.

(continued)

Table **8.2** *(continued)*

10K Schedule

	Time Goals and Daily Workouts	Special Considerations
Week 3 3	***32 to 40 minutes*** **Monday:** Recovery 1 hour to 1:15 **Tuesday:** Monofartlek (chap. 3) 20 minutes **Wednesday:** Recovery 1 hour to 1:15 **Thursday:** Recovery 45 minutes easy **Friday:** Pre's 40-30 (modified; chap. 4) 200s at 5K goal pace with fast 200 float, for 3 miles **Saturday:** Recovery 1 hour to 1:15 **Sunday:** Long run 1:30 to 2 hours ***40 to 50 minutes*** **Monday:** 40 minutes easy **Tuesday:** 15 minutes of Monofartlek **Wednesday:** 40 minutes easy **Thursday:** 40 minutes easy **Friday:** 8 × 200 meters at 5K goal pace **Saturday:** 45 minutes easy **Sunday:** 1:15 ***50 to 60 minutes*** **Monday:** 30 minutes easy **Tuesday:** Rest **Wednesday:** 30 minutes easy **Thursday:** 30 minutes easy **Friday:** Rest **Saturday:** 40 minutes easy **Sunday:** 40 minutes	Those aiming to run 50 minutes to 1 hour for their 10K will take this week easy. Jog or take some days off. Coming off of 2 hard weeks of training, your body will be crying out for a rest. Listen to it.

Table **8.2**

	Time Goals and Daily Workouts	Special Considerations
Week 4	***32 to 40 minutes*** **Monday:** Recovery 1 hour to 1:15 **Tuesday:** De Castella hills (chap. 5) **Wednesday:** Recovery 1 hour to 1:15 **Thursday:** Recovery 45 minutes easy **Friday:** Fun fartlek (chap. 3, 5) **Saturday:** Recovery 50 minutes easy **Sunday:** Long run 1:30 to 2 hours ***40 to 50 minutes*** **Monday:** 40 minutes easy **Tuesday:** Rest **Wednesday:** 40 minutes easy **Thursday:** 40 minutes easy **Friday:** Rest **Saturday:** 45 minutes easy **Sunday:** 1:15 ***50 to 60 minutes*** **Monday:** 30 minutes easy **Tuesday:** Rest **Wednesday:** 30 minutes easy **Thursday:** 30 minutes easy **Friday:** Rest **Saturday:** 40 minutes easy **Sunday:** 1 hour	If you are on a recovery run with one of those runners who insists on pushing the pace, simply turn off and go on your own loop. Make a game out of how slowly you can run. Have enough confidence in your long runs and hard days to really make your easy days very easy. It will pay off later when you are able to run better workouts. This is the way to get the most out of your training.

(continued)

187

Table **8.2** *(continued)*

10K Schedule

	Time Goals and Daily Workouts	Special Considerations
Week 5	**32 to 40 minutes** **Monday:** Recovery 1 hour to 1:15 **Tuesday:** Ric Rojas enhanced tempo run (chap. 6) **Wednesday:** Recovery 1 hour to 1:15 **Thursday:** Recovery 45 minutes easy **Friday:** Shannon Butler grass workout (chap. 2) **Saturday:** Recovery 1 hour to 1:15 **Sunday:** Long run 1:30 **40 to 50 minutes** **Monday:** 40 minutes easy **Tuesday:** Rest **Thursday:** 40 minutes easy **Friday:** Rest **Saturday:** 45 minutes easy **Sunday:** 1:20 **50 to 60 minutes** **Monday:** 30 minutes easy **Tuesday:** Rest **Wednesday:** 30 minutes easy **Thursday:** 30 minutes easy **Friday:** Rest **Saturday:** 40 minutes easy **Sunday:** 70 minutes	If you're going to wear new racing flats in your target race, buy them this week. Wear them at least a couple of times in workouts to avoid a blistery surprise on race day. Practice wearing different-thickness socks with them.

Table **8.2**

	Time Goals and Daily Workouts	Special Considerations
Week 6	***32 to 40 minutes*** **Monday:** Recovery 1 hour to 1:15 **Tuesday:** Dellinger race simulation (chap. 4) **Wednesday:** Recovery 1 hour to 1:15 **Thursday:** Recovery 1 hour **Friday:** Fartlek (chap. 3) **Saturday:** Recovery 1 hour to 1:15 **Sunday:** Long run 1:30 ***40 to 50 minutes*** **Monday:** 40 minutes easy **Tuesday:** Rest **Wednesday:** 40 minutes easy **Thursday:** 40 minutes easy **Friday:** Rest **Saturday:** 45 minutes easy **Sunday:** 1:20 ***50 to 60 minutes*** **Monday:** 30 minutes easy **Tuesday:** Rest **Wednesday:** 30 minutes easy **Thursday:** 30 minutes easy **Friday:** Rest **Saturday:** 40 minutes easy **Sunday:** 70 minutes	Make sure you get enough rest. An hour of sleep before midnight is worth 2 afterward. If you're out at a bar and your "friends" start bugging you to stay and have one more drink, politely turn them down. If they insist, tell them, "I'm an athlete. I need my rest. Let's make a deal: I'll stay for another beer with you bunch of drunks if you agree to get up and do a long run with me tomorrow morning, starting at 7 A.M."

(continued)

Table 8.2 (continued)

10K Schedule

	Time Goals and Daily Workouts	Special Considerations
Week 7	**32 to 40 minutes** **Monday:** Recovery 1 hour to 1:15 **Tuesday:** Long intervals (chap. 4); Barrios 1K repeats (6 × 1K) **Wednesday:** Recovery 1 hour to 1:15 **Thursday:** Recovery 45 minutes easy **Friday:** Grass repeats (chap. 2) 10 × 30 seconds **Saturday:** Recovery 50 minutes easy **Sunday:** Long run 1:15 **40 to 50 minutes** **Monday:** 40 minutes easy **Tuesday:** Long intervals (chap. 4); Barrios 1K repeats (4 × 1K) **Wednesday:** 40 minutes easy **Thursday:** 40 minutes easy **Friday:** Grass repeats (chap. 4) 8 × 30 seconds **Saturday:** 45 minutes easy **Sunday:** 1 hour **50 to 60 minutes** **Monday:** 30 minutes easy **Tuesday:** Long intervals (chap. 4); Barrios 1K repeats (3 × 1K) **Wednesday:** 30 minutes easy **Thursday:** 30 minutes easy **Friday:** Grass repeats (chap. 2) 6 × 30 seconds **Saturday:** 40 minutes easy **Sunday:** 40 minutes	You will not do your long run this week. Long runs can stay in your legs for a quite a while, and you don't want any excuses come race day.

Table **8.2**

	Time Goals and Daily Workouts	Special Considerations
Week 8	**_32 to 40 minutes_** **Monday:** Recovery 1 hour easy **Tuesday:** Jon Brown workout (chap. 4) **Wednesday:** Recovery 1 hour to 1:15 **Thursday:** Recovery 45 minutes easy **Friday:** Grass repeats (chap. 2) 10 × 30 seconds **Saturday:** Recovery 50 minutes easy **Sunday:** No long run **_40 to 50 minutes_** **Monday:** 40 minutes easy **Tuesday:** Rest **Wednesday:** 40 minutes easy **Thursday:** 40 minutes easy **Friday:** Grass repeats (chap. 2) 8 × 30 seconds **Saturday:** 45 minutes easy **Sunday:** 1 hour **_50 to 60 minutes_** **Monday:** 30 minutes easy **Tuesday:** Rest **Wednesday:** 30 minutes easy **Thursday:** 30 minutes easy **Friday:** Grass repeats (chap. 2) 6 × 30 seconds **Saturday:** 40 minutes easy **Sunday:** 45 minutes	This is your last hard week. If you're feeling fatigued and having trouble recovering, cut out one of your hard workouts.

(continued)

Table 8.2 (continued)

10K Schedule

	Time Goals and Daily Workouts	Special Considerations
Week 9	**32 to 40 minutes** **Monday:** Recovery 40 minutes easy **Tuesday:** 8 × grass strides slightly faster than race pace. Do not sprint or overstride. **Wednesday:** Recovery 40 minutes easy **Thursday:** Rest **Friday:** Easy jogging **Saturday:** Race **Sunday:** Long run 1:30 to 2 hours **40 to 50 minutes** **Monday:** 40 minutes easy **Tuesday:** Rest **Wednesday:** 40 minutes easy **Thursday:** Rest **Friday:** Easy jogging **Saturday:** Race **Sunday:** 1:20 **50 to 60 minutes** **Monday:** 30 minutes easy **Tuesday:** Rest **Wednesday:** 30 minutes easy **Thursday:** Rest **Friday:** Easy jogging **Saturday:** Race **Sunday:** 50 minutes	This is your taper week. Enjoy it. You've earned the rest. Don't be one of those who goes into a race overtrained and overtired. There is no better feeling for a runner than to be moving along at the start of a race feeling strong and full of running.

Marathon Program

Marathon training is similar to 10K training, but with more volume. When you are racing a marathon, the determining factor in how well you run is whether you have done the aerobic training that will allow you to cover the distance without running out of energy, or "hitting the wall."

The principle of stress and recovery is the same as in 10K and 5K training. However, in training for the marathon, your long runs take on even greater importance. Do your long runs at conversation pace. Remember to go for time on your feet, not distance. When training for the marathon, you will modify your schedule to add a semilong run on Wednesdays. This will add to your aerobic base and help give you the strength for a strong finish.

Work your way up to a standard amount of time on your long run; for most people, this will be between 2 and 2-1/2 hours on Sundays. On Wednesdays, gradually add time until you are running between 1 hour, 30 minutes and 1 hour, 45 minutes. Make these your key days, even if it means cutting back, or even skipping, your runs on other days.

Another difference: Before a marathon, take a 2-week taper. It's hard to do, but some elite runners say that none of the training you do the 2 weeks before a race is going to help you for that race (although it will, of course, help you down the road). You will most likely not run more than two marathons a year; make sure you go into yours 100 percent ready to race.

The ingredients for many top marathoners, such as U.S. Olympian Mark Coogan and Australians Rob de Castella, Steve Moneghetti, and Shaun Creighton, are two long runs a week, Sunday and Wednesday; three hard sessions, Tuesday, Thursday, and Saturday; and two recovery days, Monday and Friday.

Frank Shorter was a bit different. His long run was on Sunday, with three hard sessions Monday, Wednesday, and Friday, and three recovery days Tuesday, Thursday, and Saturday.

The commonality is that for all these world-class athletes, it took years of uninterrupted training to build up to that schedule. Shorter once figured out that he averaged more than 100 miles a week, every week, for 17 years. De Castella averaged more than 120 miles a week for 10 years, missing a total of just 15 days of training during that time. That's the kind of consistency that makes champions.

For most of you, one long run per week will be enough, with two hard sessions and 4 recovery days. In general, the length of your long run will vary depending on the time of year and whether you are building up for a race. By doing the long run every week (or twice a week), you will always be building your aerobic base. And with the hard sessions you will always be working on your speed and endurance. Creighton puts it this way: "You're never far away from your base, and never far away from your speed."

And that means, you hope, that you are never far away from running a good marathon.

Table **8.3**

Marathon Schedule

	Daily Workouts	Special Considerations
Week 1	**Monday:** Recovery 45 minutes to 1:15 **Tuesday:** Lorraine Moller 2-mile repeats (chap. 6) *×3 132* **Wednesday:** Medium-long 1:15 to 1:30 **Thursday:** Recovery 45 minutes to 1 hour easy **Friday:** De Castella 400-meter *×14* workout (chap. 4) *92 82secs* **Saturday:** Recovery 50 minutes easy **Sunday:** Long run 1:45 to 2:15	The key to marathon running is being able to produce enough energy to sustain you through the distance, says Olympic marathon bronze medalist Lorraine Moller. "The biggest mistake I see is people training anaerobically for a race that is 99 percent aerobic. I find that one of my principal roles as a coach is telling people to slow down and take it easy during training because athletes are highly motivated people and have a tendency to overdo it."
Week 2	**Monday:** Recovery 1:00 to 1:15 **Tuesday:** Rod DeHaven AT run (chap. 6) *142* **Wednesday:** Medium-long run 1:15 to 1:45 **Thursday:** Recovery 45 minutes easy **Friday:** 8 × 400 meters with a 200-meter float **Saturday:** Recovery 1:00 to 1:15 **Sunday:** Long run 2 hours to 2:15	When basketball player Michael Jordan was winning six NBA titles, he often said he was successful because he let the game come to him within the framework of Phil Jackson's triangle offense. Jordan did not force his shots. So it is with running. Don't get impatient and try to rush your marathon preparation. Rather, let it come to you within the framework of your training schedule. Stay healthy, stay consistent, and you will improve.
Week 3	**Monday:** Recovery 1 hour easy **Tuesday:** Rod DeHaven AT run (chap. 6) *142* **Wednesday:** Medium-long run 1:30 to 1:45 **Thursday:** Recovery 45 minutes to 1 hour easy **Friday:** Interval workout (chap. 4) **Saturday:** Recovery 1 hour to 1:15 **Sunday:** Long run 2:15	The most efficient way to increase your aerobic fitness is through your long run. You might be tempted to skimp on your long runs; don't do it, says Rob de Castella. "Long runs are the hardest part of training to do, and the Sunday long run was the most important part of my training."

Table **8.3**

	Daily Workouts	**Special Considerations**
Week 4	**Monday:** Recovery 1 hour easy **Tuesday:** Rod DeHaven AT run (chap. 6) **Wednesday:** Medium-long run 1:30 to 1:45 **Thursday:** Recovery 45 minutes to 1 hour easy **Friday:** Interval workout (chap. 4) **Saturday:** Recovery 50 minutes easy **Sunday:** Long run 3 to 3-1/2 hours	This week you'll do an extra-long run, to get you used to going beyond the time you will be on your feet in the marathon. Doing this 6 weeks before your marathon gives you enough time to recover from the pounding your legs will take. Can't afford a massage after this extra-long run? Try soaking your legs in a cold creek or lake, or even a bathtub of ice and cold water. This is known as a poor man's massage.
Week 5	**Monday:** Recovery 30 minutes or day off if tired from Sunday run **Tuesday:** Rod DeHaven AT run (chap. 6) **Wednesday:** Medium-long run 1:30 to 1:45 **Thursday:** Recovery 45 minutes to 1 hour easy **Friday:** Interval workout (chap. 4) **Saturday:** Recovery 50 minutes easy **Sunday:** Long run 2:15	"Hydrate or die!" That might sound a little extreme, but it is accurate. Hydrating on long runs will give you practice drinking while running. You can either carry water with you, place bottles the night before in strategic spots, or quickly find out who your friends are by asking them to bike or drive alongside you with fluids.
Week 6	**Monday:** Recovery 1 hour easy **Tuesday:** Rod DeHaven AT run (chap. 6) **Wednesday:** Medium-long run 1:30 to 1:45 **Thursday:** Recovery 45 minutes to 1 hour easy **Friday:** Grass workout, 5 × 5 minutes hard **Saturday:** Recovery 1 hour to 1:15 **Sunday:** Long run 2:15 minutes	Do your AT run on the same course if possible. You should see some improvement as the weeks go by. If you're feeling a bit sluggish on this or any other workout, cut back a bit on your weekly volume. Instead of worrying about hitting a set number of miles each week, focus on doing excellent workouts and staying on top of your running.

(continued)

Table **8.3** *(continued)*

Marathon Schedule

	Daily Workouts	Special Considerations
Week 7	**Monday:** Recovery 1 hour easy **Tuesday:** Hill workout (chap. 6) **Wednesday:** Medium-long run 1:30 to 1:45 **Thursday:** Recovery 45 minutes to 1 hour easy **Friday:** Workout from chapter 4 **Saturday:** Recovery 50 minutes easy **Sunday:** Long run 2:15	The "no pain, no gain" attitude some coaches espouse does not always lead to the best training regimen. You need to work hard, and work consistently, but every workout does not have to be an epic session. You have to train within the general parameters of your current strength and fitness levels.
Week 8	**Monday:** Recovery 1 hour easy **Tuesday:** Any AT workout (chap. 6) **Wednesday:** Medium-long run 1:30 to 1:45 **Thursday:** Recovery 45 minutes to 1 hour easy **Friday:** 8 × 30 seconds on grass workout (chap. 2) **Saturday:** Recovery 1 hour to 1:15 **Sunday:** Long run 2:15	Do 6 to 10 strides after some of your recovery runs, even when training for the marathon. This will help you learn to change your pace and will help you finish your intervals and races faster.
Week 9	**Monday:** Recovery 1 hour easy **Tuesday:** Reduced fartlek workout **Wednesday:** Recovery 1 hour **Thursday:** Recovery 45 minutes to 1 hour easy **Friday:** Reduced workout **Saturday:** Recovery 50 minutes easy **Sunday:** Long run 1:15	At this point in your training, 2 weeks before your marathon, you should focus on recovering. Go to bed early. Eat well. Begin backing off on your training by cutting out the Wednesday medium-long run and reducing the length of your Sunday run.
Week 10	**Monday:** Recovery 1 hour easy **Tuesday:** Reduced fartlek workout **Wednesday:** 50 minutes easy, followed by strides **Thursday:** 45 minutes **Friday:** Rest **Saturday:** Jog **Sunday:** Race	Stay humble. No matter how well you're running, or how successful you are, keep in the back of your mind what Steve Jones said after setting the world record in Chicago in 1984: "Every runner is just a hamstring injury away from oblivion."

Workouts

1   **Long Runs: Building a Base**   **I**

Magnolia Never Lies	Mark Wetmore	4
Waiatarua Hills	Arthur Lydiard	6
The Cascade-Fourth Street Loop	Frank Shorter	8
Woodhill Forest Long Run	Dick Quax	10
Sandia Peak 18-Miler	David Morris	12
Treadmill Long Run	Kim Jones	14
The Dudley Long Run	Mike Dudley	15
27-Mile Overdistance Run	Kathrine Switzer	16
Hidden Hills 21-Miler		
(a Boston Simulation)	Benji Durden	18

2   **Off-Road Training: Sparing Your Legs**   **21**

Shorter's Grass Repeats	Frank Shorter	24
Royal Air Force Repeats	Steve Jones	26
Colleen and Bobby McGee	Colleen De Reuck	28
Montana Cone to Cone	Shannon Butler	30
Carr's Cross Country Simulation	Donna Garcia	32
The Rock Creek 10-Miler	Deena Drossin	34
Alamosa Miles	Joe Vigil	36
Race Pace Mile Repeats	Steve Plasencia	38
Lawson's Race Tempo Workout	Jerry Lawson	40
Emil's 100 × 400 Meters	Emil Zatopek	42
Plaatjes' Marathon Indicator	Mark Plaatjes	44
Radcliffe's Off-Road 2K Reps	Paula Radcliffe	46

3   **Fartlek Training: Mixing it Up**   **49**

The "Mono" Fartlek Workout	Shaun Creighton	52
LeMay's 10-Mile Icebreaker	Joe LeMay	55
Vale of Glamorgan Fartlek	Steve Jones	56
Holmenkollen and Sognsvann		
Forest Fartlek	Dave Welch	58
The Army Short Fartlek	Jason Stewart	60
Meyer-Rodgers Fartlek	Bill Rodgers	61
Coogan's Marathon Strength Workout	Mark Coogan	62
The Wolfpack Fartlek	Rich Castro	64
Kardong's Road Fartlek	Don Kardong	66

4 **Interval Workouts: The Need for Speed** **69**

Masback's Mitochondrial Change of Pace	Craig Masback	72
10 × 10K	Arturo Barrios	74
Guerra's Confidence Builder	Silvio Guerra	76
Pre's 30-40 Workout:		
Advanced Interval Training	Bill Dellinger	78
300-Meter Intervals	Libbie Hickman	81
The Alberto Salazar Special	Marc Davis	82
Wetmore's Secret Intervals		
(or 5K Goal Pace 500s)	Adam Goucher	84
Kenahs' Key Workout	Rich Kenah/Cheri Kenah	86
Rainey's 300s	Merideth Rainey Valmon	88
Hogen's Pyramid	Dieter Hogen	90
World-Record Kilometers	Khalid Khannouchi	91
400s With a Fast Float	Rob de Castella	92
Holman's 600s	Steve Holman	94
Repeat 800s	Frank Shorter	96
Brown's Championship Simulation Run	Jon Brown	98
Culpepper's Ladder	Shayne Culpepper	100
Bannister's Quarters	Sir Roger Bannister	102
Tegen's "Emptying the Anaerobic		
Credit Card"	Suzy Favor Hamilton	104

5 **Hill Workouts: Building Strength and Stamina** **107**

Masback's Ski Area Bounding	Craig Masback	109
Deek's Thursday Hill Session	Rob de Castella	110
Sinclair's "Money Workout"	Jon Sinclair	112
Wall Street 10-Miler	Melody Fairchild	114
Carpenter's Perfect 20-Minute Workout	Matt Carpenter	116
Agony Hill	Kip Keino	118
Fluorspar Hill	Moses Tanui	120
The Circuit	Peter Snell	122

6 **Tempo Runs: Pushing the Threshold** **125**

Track AT 10K	Alan Culpepper	128
Rojas' 6K Enhanced Anaerobic		
Threshold Workout	Ric Rojas	130
Moller's 2-Milers	Lorraine Moller	132
Oregon Sustained Run	Damien Koch	134

The Michigan Miles	Ron Warhurst	136
Da Costa's 5Ks	Ronaldo Da Costa	138
Mykotok's 4-Miler	Michael Mykotok	139
10-Mile Tempo Run	Craig Young	140
Alamosa Tempo Run	Peter De La Cerda	141
DeHaven's Arboretum Run	Rod DeHaven	142
Dowling's Building Block Tempo Runs	Keith Dowling	144
Somers' Run of Alternating 400 Meters	Linda Somers-Smith	146
Simon Says: 10K Repeats	Lidia Simon	147

7

Recovery Fun: Rejuvenating With Play **149**

Freddy's Hoof and Bike	Don "Freddy" Fredericks	152
Fun Recovery Run	Peter Julian	154
Running of the Dice	Aaron Berthold	156
Kill Your Partner—If You Can	Roland Vera and Silvio Guerra	158
Stinkers	Scott Winston	160
Park-to-Park Fartlek	Andy Aiken	162

About the Author

Michael Sandrock combines 15 years of experience as an award-winning sport journalist with a quarter-century of running expertise. His first book, *Running with the Legends,* marked Sandrock as an expert and upcoming star in the field of sport literature. He currently covers running for the *Daily Camera* newspaper in Boulder, Colorado, and maintains freelance status with numerous publications, including *Running Times, Runner's World, Marathon & Beyond,* and *Trail Runner.* He is also a member of the Colorado Press Association, where he has won several accolades for Best Sports Story of the Year.

As a runner, Sandrock has trained with many elite athletes and Olympic champions, with personal bests of 2:24:00 in the marathon and 30:23 in the 10K. He holds a master's degree from the University of Colorado and varsity letters in cross country and track. Sandrock has coached high school track and has also coached overseas for the U.S. Information Agency.

Albert "Big Rock" Sandrock

Sandrock currently resides in Boulder, where he runs, writes, and manages the Shoes for Africa project, which he founded. This program donates new and used equipment to underprivileged athletes around the world. Tax-deductible donations can be mailed to P.O. Box 2223, Boulder, CO 80306. You can contact the author at sandrockm@thedailycamera.com.

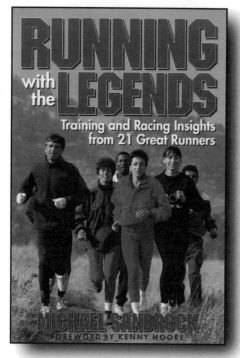